Tears of Blood

Tears of Blood

A true story as told by

Maria Evereta

Authored by
Gérard Desjardins

GREY DIAMOND BOOKS

In memory of

Fanélie (Fanny) Casimir
1933 – 1967

Who passed away in Haiti, on December 23rd 1967. She was 34 years old at her untimely death and she left six small children behind...

When Angels cry, they shed tears of blood. When Fanny died, they cried for what was to come...

AUTHOR'S NOTE

This book was written with the sole purpose of exposing unheard-of cruelties that at times are inflicted upon innocent women and children in the world.

Let not the reader be fooled for there are many incidents that occur, and this sometimes in one's own back yard, that merit intervention by any decent human being. To turn one's head and pretend that one doesn't hear or see what is happening renders the unseeing pretender as guilty as the perpetrator.

To not lend a helping hand to a fellow human being in need, *when it is possible*, is totally unacceptable in this day and age. When we are blessed in being able to live in such a generous and wealthy environment, it is unacceptable to let anyone go without food when our stomachs are full. Think for one minute... What if the situation were reversed? What would you like the other person to do?

Think of the old biblical saying; *"Do onto other as you would have them do onto you"*. Apply this rule religiously and the world will be a better place to live in.

The writing of this book was made possible by events that took place during the past eighty years and unlikely circumstances where perfect strangers met.

The names of some people, villages or cities mentioned in this book may have been changed and this in order to maintain a certain amount of privacy for the seven main characters of the story that were still alive at the publication date of this book.

Apart from factual - Resemblance of any characters in this book to anyone living or dead is coincidental.

ACKNOWLEDGMENTS

My heartfelt thanks to every one who had a part in the completion of this book, particularly Maria Evereta who had the courage and determination to bring to light her own tragic life story and that of her mother's perilous life journey here on Earth. I also thank every member of the family, *mentioned in this story*, who allowed me the privilege of sharing with them some of the troubling experiences they had to endure and suffer a long time ago. To those who shared old photos from their albums, a special thank you.

I can't help but wonder if someone from beyond the grave has caused events to happen which resulted in exposing the unjust treatment inflicted upon innocent people at different times of their lives. Maybe someone *'long gone from this present dimension of time'* wanted her story to be told in order to rest in peace.

If this is so, I thank that dear departed person for allowing her Soul to intertwine with mine as I feel like I was there and lived those painful moments with her. I also thank her for allowing me the privilege of bringing her story to print.

A special mention and thanks to the ever Great Architect up above, who makes all things possible, and to my special and kind Guardian Angel who takes care of me and my loved ones.

Contents

– A Chance Meeting –

During the month of June in 2001, the author was at a posh Chicago hotel attending a business meeting. Following that morning meeting, he sat in the hotel lounge enjoying a cup of coffee as he chatted with an old friend who was in charge of security at the hotel.

At the same time, *in the lounge*, there was a young Black woman sitting there having some coffee. She was beautiful, had a great smile and was wearing a hotel uniform. "Who is that beautiful lady?" *inquired the author*. "That's Maria," *replied the friend*, "she is in charge of the chamber maids at the hotel."

The author asked his friend if he could be introduced and the friend invited the lady to their table. There; a lengthy conversation began between the author and the lady who would one day become the teller of this story.

Over the years, a real friendship developed between the two and the author couldn't help but notice that there was something buried in that woman's mind. She would often seem to drift off to another place. She at times looked like she had mentally gone elsewhere while still physically being with the author.

With time and patience, the author got this Creole lady to open up and discuss the secrets she kept hidden deep in her mind, which in turn kept haunting her each and every day, year after year.

She had never dared to tell anyone else about the horrible experiences that she and her four brothers, sister and aunt were forced to endure in order for them to survive a hell on earth in Haiti.

This book is the result of that unexpected meeting ten years ago, where two strangers met and with time became best friends, Soul mates and life partners.

Brief history of Haiti

Haiti is a country in the Caribbean, occupying the western part of the island of Hispaniola: pop (est.1990) 6,500,000; official languages, Haitian Creole, French; capital, Port-au-Prince. The western third of Hispaniola was ceded to France by Spain in 1697. The French already had settlements there, established by pirates, and after 1697 many slaves were imported from West Africa to work on sugar plantations. In 1791 the slaves rose in rebellion under Toussaint L'Ouverture and other leaders, and in 1804 the colony was proclaimed an independent state under the name of Haiti. It was the second country in the Americas (after the US) to achieve freedom from colonial rule. Haiti was administered by the US (1915-34) after a succession of corrupt dictatorships. From 1957 to 1986 the country was under the oppressive dictatorship of the Duvalier family. The overthrow of Jean-Claude Duvalier in 1986 was followed, in 1990, by the election of Jean-Bertrand Aristide (b.1953) as Haiti's first democratically chosen President, but in the following year the military seized power. In 1994 the US sent troops to Haiti in an attempt to ensure the restoration of democracy. On January 12, 2010 the capital of Haiti was hit with by a massive earthquake that killed hundreds of thousands of Haitians. Most of Port-au-Prince was destroyed and the presidential palace was severely damaged. In April of 2011 following a disputed election, Michel Martelly *(formally known as the popular musician, Sweet Micky)* was elected as the legitimate president of Haiti...

Prologue

There were strange things happening within an area surrounding a small Haitian village situated close to the Dominican Republic. Young boys aged between seven and twelve were being found murdered along deserted pathways leading to and from Quanamainte. These poor Souls were decapitated and this for no apparent reason.

Some days you would only find one dead boy. Other days there were as much as three decapitated bodies found and the odd day none were found. These events were proving to be of great distraught for the women who wondered if their own sons would be next.

There were never any young girls or adults killed, only boys aged between seven and twelve.

Added to those troubling and unexplained murders, the people of Quanamainte were poor and in need. Food had become a rare commodity and more than half of the villagers were starving. There was a lot of hardship in many parts of Haiti during that period of time. We were in the spring of the year 1938.

It eventually became known that masked vigilantes were killing these boys because they blamed them for the overpopulation, which was causing all of the poverty in the villages. If they killed off the young boys there would be fewer young men and less pregnancies in the future thus reducing the main cause of the poverty!

Prologue

One has to wonder if the real reason the vigilantes were killing off those young boys were not but a ploy to keep the supply of young girls available for their own personal lust and bestial pleasures.

In this and many other parts of the world, women were considered inferior to the men of the villages. Most of the village people had little or no schooling and most of the men treated their women like cattle.

A man only had one first wife and God forbid should any man touch another man's first wife as this could lead to fights that often caused death between rivals.

However, apart from his legal or first wife, it was considered proper and acceptable for any man to have as many women and families as his male stamina could permit. To see a man with six wives and twenty or more children was common and non-surprising. This type of man was even admired by other men even though they never properly provided for their *"legitimate"* children.

In other parts of Haiti were poverty was of no issue, both men and women were properly educated and much better off financially. The women of these men were treated with respect and violent behavior on the part of men was not well looked upon. Those well to do men were much more discreet and any mistresses were kept far away and secret and the same applied to off-springs. In the bigger townships and cities, the children went to the best schools and became doctors, lawyers, businessmen and politician of course.

To find a man with many women and children in those well to do places was rare indeed and there was no killing of the boys in those areas either. No! The killing sprees were reserved for the poor and destitute families that lived in the slums and ghettos of Haiti ...

- 1 -
The Beginning

It was April 7th 1938 and a young boy named Brutus stood in the schoolyard close to Quanamainte, a small village bordering the Dominican Republic. The village was situated some two or three hours drive away from Port-au-Prince, the capital of Haiti.

That particular day was Brutus' tenth birthday, but there wasn't any reason for celebrations as rumors were circulating that the vigilantes were off on another killing spree. Brutus was scared and had a gut feeling that his time on earth was nearing completion if he didn't get away from this hellhole in Haiti.

There was an eleven years old girl in Brutus' class and the two were close friends. He asked her to take off her dress and lend it to him so that he could disguise himself as a girl in order to get back home safely. The classmate knew of the senseless killings going on and understood why Brutus was scared.

She agreed to lend him her dress and the scarf she was wearing to cover his head. She also advised him to take a basket from the teacher's desk, for placing that basket on his arm would make the disguise foolproof thus assuring him safe passage home.

She went into the classroom, got the basket and some old clothing to wear and she then gave her own clothing with the basket to Brutus and left him there.

Tears of Blood

Brutus watched as his classmate went on her way but he knew that he would most probably never see her again. Brutus had another plan and it was not going back home. He rolled up his trousers as high as they would go up on his legs, put on the dress and scarf, and with the basket on his arm he made his way to the market place instead of home.

Once arrived at the market place he was safe for the time being. He removed the dress and scarf and asked a merchant if he needed help to load-up his truck. The merchant told him that he could use the help but that he would only pay one dollar, plus he had to come along with the truck to Port-au-Prince to help unload the merchandise. Brutus was jubilant and agreed to the merchant's proposal at once. His luck had changed '*he thought to himself*', not only am I safe, but I am on my way to Port-au-Prince.

As the truck left the market place for Port-au-Prince, Brutus looked back and watched until he could no longer see the market place or the village that he would never return to or forget. During the drive to the big city, he thought of his mother and father. What would they say when their son never returned home. Of course they would think he was dead, another victim of the vigilantes. This excitement had tired him and he fell asleep only to wake up when the merchant shook him and shouted, "*wake up it's time to unload the truck.*"

Once his work completed, Brutus collected his dollar in wages and told the merchant that he would not be returning to Quanamainte. Brutus felt somewhat lost. Here he was in a strange city with no friends or family. He had a dollar to his name and no place to stay. He was like a stray dog on the streets of Port-au-Prince. But at least he was safe for the time being.

The Beginning

The dollar he had was soon gone and hunger set in. For days he lived on the streets and waterfront begging for food. But this would not be as easy a task as it seemed because the good places to beg, *such as busy streets and good street corners*, were already being used by other homeless children.

On top of that problem, the other homeless children were teamed up in groups of three or four making sure that, *together*, they could hold onto their ground and keep a control over the good spots to be begging.

Also when it rained or when it was cold, Brutus was not welcomed in spots that other groups of children had already turned into make shift homes for themselves. Brutus had to be content with finding a suitable porch to hide under or an abandoned garage where he could shelter himself from the wind, rain and cold.

Many times Brutus was punched in the face and kicked for trying to move into some of the spots held by other homeless kids. So for many months Brutus found out what it meant to be alone and forgotten on the streets and waterfront of Port-au-Prince.

This went on for many months until one day, when; a stranger got him work shinning shoes and washing cars on the waterfront. His new life had begun. He did this for three years, *always living,* on the streets of Port-au-Prince.

When days were good and he got jobs shinning shoes and washing cars then he had money to eat and to buy the odd piece of clothing. But he always had to watch his back so that the other kids didn't steal his hard earned money.

This style of living would go on for three years and Brutus believed that this would now be his way of life.

Tears of Blood

Then; *when he was thirteen*, his luck changed for the better. In exchange for food and a place to stay he got a job as a watchman in a garage that repaired cars.

At night he would watch over the cars in the garage and by doing that he had a place to stay. He no longer lived on the streets of Port-au-Prince. He had a place to sleep without worrying about the rain or the cold and had the necessary food to survive. This was a hell of a lot better than living in Quanamainte, *'he would think to himself.'*

Brutus had now learned how to suck up to people and make them like him and even feel sorry for him. He would always bend over backwards to be of service to the mechanics. He would always have kind words for them and complimented them whenever an occasion would arise.

This behavior, *on Brutus' part,* earned him rewards from the mechanics. At times they would give him some clothes or shoes and would even tip him when he helped with some of the basic repairs. With time and being genuinely friendly with all of the garage workers he ended up being a full time helper to the mechanics.

This in turn would lead him to starting and moving cars for those same mechanics. Brutus was a very intelligent boy and before you knew it, he had learned how to drive cars. He was driving the cars in and out of the garage for the mechanics and even the clients.

One day, a client who had taken a liking to Brutus was having his car repaired at the garage. He told Brutus that he should not be sleeping in a garage and working without compensation. The client was a well to do gentleman named Eli Joseph and he offered Brutus real work as a yard boy at his residence.

The Beginning

His duties as yard boy consisted of watering the plants, washing his new master's car, sweeping and keeping the exterior of the residence clean to the liking of his new boss, Eli Joseph.

After having proven himself worthy, he was given a small salary. Further on he was given the privilege of screening guest and opening the front door so those guest could enter and meet with the master of the house.

He was now parking the guests' cars and running errands in town with Eli Joseph's car. The more time went by the more importance he got within the master's favor.

In exchange for his services, he now had a small room in the yard to live in, he was being fed three meals a day, had a place to sleep, a basic salary, and all of his clothing was supplied by his master.

By now he was able to drive a car rather well. Each time Brutus would run errands in town for the master, he would make sure to meet and talk with as many new people as possible.

Being well dressed and driving a fancy car certainly got him a lot of attention and before he knew it, he had made many new friends in town.

When he had an evening off, he would visit the local soda shop and have drinks and ice cream with the many friends that now surrounded him. He shared and heard many stories with his newfound friends, but he never talked about his hurried exit from Quanamainte.

He no longer was that homeless boy from three years ago. *Without realizing it*, all of what happened would lead to better things for him in the near future.

Tears of Blood

(Meanwhile during that same time period in another part of Haiti, there was a small village situated on top of a mountain where a different scenario was taking place.

The village was called Diquiny and it was situated some thirty or so minutes of drive from Port-au-Prince.

In this village there was a young girl named Fania. She was nine years old at the time and little did she know what horrors and misery fate had in store for her during the next twenty-five years of her life.

Fania's mother had thirteen children, five daughters and eight sons. Being of a poor family, when the girls were old enough, they would be sent to Port-au-Prince to work as house domestics.

The girls had to tend for themselves, as there was no other way to survive in Haiti when you were a girl born into a poor family.

At the young age of twelve, Fania was sent on her way to Port-au-Prince. Once there, she would begin working as a house domestic for a Madame Casimir.

Possibly Fania's mother had chosen that particular lady because they both had the same family names. However the two families were not related in any way.

At that same time period, Brutus was still at the service of Eli Joseph, when; the master passed away thus leaving Brutus with no job and no place to live...

The Beginning

During the previous three years, Brutus had made many friends and one day, one of those friends brought him to a gaming house.

As Brutus was without work, he would always be at the gaming house gambling which in turn led him to meet and become friends with, *Gisele*, the daughter of the man who owned the gambling house.

Months later and still being without work Brutus, *with Gisele at his side for luck*, could always to be found at the tables gambling.

The gaming friendship established between Brutus and Gisele, eventually led to the two becoming sweethearts and lovers. One day Gisele discovered that she was pregnant with Brutus' child.

When Gisele's father heard of the situation, he told Brutus, *in no gentle words*, to find a job and to face his responsibilities, and to do right by Gisele and his child that she was carrying.

Brutus knew very well that the owner of the gaming house was not a man to be reckoned with, *specially*, when his daughter was involved. So he asked Gisele to help him find some work so that they could get a place to stay together and bring up their coming child.

Gisele took Brutus to a voodoo priest to seek help in finding her partner a job. The voodoo priest did a ritual ceremony and instructed Brutus to watch for a stranger that would approach him in seven days. That stranger would take him to a place where he would find work.

Brutus was to follow that stranger without saying one word to him. The priest warned that absolutely no verbal communication of any sort was to be undertaken between himself and the stranger. Seven days later a stranger approached Brutus and signaled him to follow.

Tears of Blood

The stranger led Brutus to the Liberian Embassy then he turned and walked away without saying a word.

Brutus turned and glanced at the strange man that was walking away. That was the weirdest man he had ever met *'he thought to himself'*. The man looked like he was in a trance and his eyes showed no emotions whatsoever. The guy looked like a bloody zombie. But here he was in front of the Liberian Embassy wondering what the hell this place could have in store for a poor village man like himself.

He gathered up his courage and made his way up the stairway to the Embassy's front entrance and boldly walked in. There he saw what being rich was all about.

There was a huge chandelier hanging in the entrance and beautiful oil paintings on the walls. His shoes sank in the plush carpets that lined the entrance floor. He never knew that such richness and beauty existed.

He walked over to a desk where a beautiful well-dressed lady was seated and he introduced himself. The lady was the Embassy secretary and you passed by her before you could see or talk to anyone in the Embassy.

He told the secretary that he was married and that his woman was expecting and that he would be glad to take any job that was available. She asked him what qualifications he had. Brutus replied that he could do gardening and take care of cars. He assured the secretary that he could do any kind of hard labor work.

After some reflection, the secretary asked him if he could drive a car as the Ambassador needed a chauffeur to drive him around. Brutus told her that he was a very good driver with a lot of experience. So the secretary had Brutus meet the ambassador. Following a short conversation with the ambassador, Brutus got the job...

The Beginning

He couldn't believe what had just happened. An hour ago he was unemployed and without a place to stay and added to this, he had a pregnant woman to take care of. Now he was employed in a well paying job that anyone would cut off their right arm to have.

Brutus had never believed in voodoo priests before but his opinion had now changed drastically. He now saw his woman in another perspective. Gisele had many powerful friends and she was not a person to fool with.

He went at once to rent an apartment, then to the gaming house to pick up Gisele. Later that night, they moved into their home to begin their new family life.

He explained to Gisele what his duties were at the Embassy. Of course the first priority would be driving the Ambassador around and keeping the Ambassador's car spotless. One of his other tasks was to go two times a week to the Casimir general store in town and pick-up supplies needed for the Embassy.

At twenty years old, young Brutus had established himself as a working family man of some importance.

He then decided to return to the village he had run away from ten years ago. He would visit with his family and friends for a few days. A long time had passed and no one recognized him in Quanamainte.

His mother and father had always believed that those vigilantes had murdered him ten years ago. Everyone was jubilant to see him alive and well.

Brutus stayed for a few days reminiscing with his family and his old friends from childhood.

One week later he returned to Port-au-Prince, his new job at the Liberian Embassy, and to his new life with Gisele who had been anxiously awaiting his return.

- 2 -

The Deception

While Brutus got settled into his job working at the Embassy, a young girl named Fania was busy working at the Casimir general store in Point-au-Prince.

Fania was that young girl that had left the village of Diquini three years ago, when she was twelve years old.

She had worked as a domestic for Madame Casimir for the past three years. When she had reached the age of fifteen, she had been given other duties to perform at the store such as; filling and weighing bags of sugar and flour, bottling pickles and oil and various other small tasks...

Several times a week Brutus would visits the general store to buy the goods required for the Embassy. Brutus soon took notice of the young and beautiful Fania and, *for personal reasons*, introduced himself as Severe thus keeping secret his real name and the fact that he had another woman and child.

Brutus would often flirt with Fania telling her how beautiful a woman she was and so on. He would often take her to town for ice cream and sodas at the local soda parlor. Soon they were taking walks together and holding hands.

After one year of carrying on a friendly relationship the couple became sweethearts. One night, while they sat cuddling in the Embassy car, Brutus took Fania for the first time and they became lovers from then on.

Tears of Blood

During all of this time, Fania had no idea of who really was, and she was convinced that he lived at the Embassy where he worked.

Fania was then seventeen years old and madly in love with Sever, *who in fact was Brutus the family man*.

They made love several times a week until one day, *much to her dismay*, Fania discovered that she was pregnant and didn't know what to do about it.

She hadn't heard from Severe in over a week so she decided to tell Madame Casimir and ask her for advice.

After having explained her condition and problem to Madame Casimir, *and being that Madame Casimir was responsible for her domestic's well being,* she ordered Fania to have Severe come over to the house at once to discuss the delicate situation with her.

While all this was going on at the Casimir residence, Severe *(Brutus)'* other woman, Gisele, had discovered that she in turn was pregnant with a second child. Gisele now had one son, *the firstborn called Jean*, and a second child on the way.

When Severe was informed of the situation by Fania and upon hearing that Madame Casimir wanted to meet and talk with him, he realized that he was in trouble.

His first wife Gisele's father, *who held the gambling house*, was by no means a person to be reckoned with and Madame Casimir who personally knew the Liberian Ambassador could not easily be put off either.

Severe had very little choice. He had to keep his double life a secret or face dire consequences.

The next day, Severe went to meet with Madame Casimir and after a serious discussion agreed to become engaged to Fania his seemingly newfound love.

The Deception

In the days and weeks that followed, Madame Casimir began making all the arrangements for the wedding. She had a wedding dress made up for Fania, reserved a church date, a reception hall and even booked a choir for the church ceremony.

Then arrangements were made for Fania's mother and father to come to Port-au-Prince to meet Severe *(Brutus)* their future son in law. They would also help with the preparation of food that would be required to feed the guests that would be invited to the wedding.

Fania's parents arrived at Madame Casimir's home in Port-au-Prince, one week before the wedding date. They helped with the decorations of the reception hall and took care of cooking all of the Haitian rice that would be needed to feed the one hundred and fifty guests that confirmed their attendance to the wedding.

Come the wedding day, all the invited guests and family were at the church ready for the ceremony. Fania was absolutely beautiful in her white dress as she stood at the church alter nervously awaiting the arrival of Sever, her husband to be.

The wedding was scheduled for 5 p.m. and it was already 6 p.m. and Severe had not yet arrived at the church. The priest waited for another 30 minutes but still no sign of Severe. By 7 p.m. it became obvious that Severe would not show up thus leaving Fania standing alone and abandoned at the church alter.

Nonetheless, Madame Casimir invited the shocked guests to the reception hall, where food, *having been previously prepared*, was waiting for them.

Fania was hysterical as her parents took her back to the Casimir residence. There the three held each other and cried together for what seemed to be an eternity.

Tears of Blood

The next day Fania's parents hugged and kissed their daughter one more time before leaving Port-au-Prince and returning home to their village in Diquiny.

Madame Casimir was furious, as she could not have a pregnant housekeeper working for her. She told Fania that she was fired and would have to move.

Fania was only given 30 days to get out and find somewhere else to live.

Having not seen or heard of Severe *(Brutus)* for a full month, Fania became completely discouraged.

With no money, four months pregnant and no place to live, she decided to confront Severe at the Liberian Embassy and explain to him the dire situation that she was faced with.

When she met him, she asked him why had he done that to her? Why did he stand her up at the church alter in front of all the guest and family?

Severe told her that he was sick that day and that he could not marry without the presence of his family.

Fania was totally discouraged and asked him what she should do in her situation.

Severe proposed that he rent her a room to stay and that they would marry after the birth of the child.

That evening Fania left Madame Casimir's home and moved into the small room Severe had rented for her. For once Severe had seemed to keep his word!

After being installed in her room for a week, she discovered that Severe only came and slept over every second night. When questioned about his strange behavior, Sever told her that his duties at the Embassy call for him to be out of town every second day.

The Deception

In Haiti, It was *(and most probably still is)* normal practice for women not to question their men as to their behavior. Upsetting their men could lead to the women receiving serious beatings and/or even worse, outright abandonment.

In Haiti, men do what they want when they want to and the poor defenseless women must accept that principle without question or face the consequences.

Fania was not pleased with the situation but being in her condition, total submission was the only way.

During the next four hard months of her pregnancy, Severe would stay-over every second night demanding sex from her. Whether she felt like it or not was totally irrelevant. If she felt sick that didn't mater either.

Once in a while he would beat her for no apparent reason. Most Haitian women believe that; *when men beat them*, it's a sign of love. It means that the men love them!

In North America a man goes to jail for beating his wife, but not in Haiti. Why? Because it's a sign of love!!!

How can women anywhere in the world have such a misconception of love is beyond understanding.

One month later, *at the general hospital,* Fania gave birth to her first born, a son named Sergio.

The next day, Severe and one of his friends named Anna, visited Fania at the hospital to see the baby.

When Anna saw the child she was amazed and said to Fania *"My God; Brutus' children all resemble him!"*

Fania's eyes opened wide for she didn't understand what Anna had just said to her. What are you talking about shouted Fania? ***"And who in hell is Brutus?"***

Tears of Blood

Anna explains to her, that Severe's real name was Brutus, and that he had two other children with another woman named Gisele.

Fania had a fit and asked Brutus why he gave her a false name. She understood at once why Brutus didn't show up at the wedding and why he only stayed over every second night.

She realized there and then; that life for her, *from that day on,* would be hell on Earth.

Brutus, furious that the truth had come out and that he could not justify any plausible answer, stormed out of the hospital with Anna, leaving Fania in tears and in complete despair.

He only returned two days later to take his woman and child out of the hospital and bring them to the little room that they called home.

Even with all of those deceptions, Fania still had love in her heart for the man who had deceived her and who had taken her innocence away. Was Brutus some kind of an evil person, *she wondered,* and what were his plans for her and her son's future?

Now having everything under control, Brutus carried on with his old habits of being with Fania one night, and with Gisele the next. At that point Gisele was starting to have doubts about her own man, *but being Haitian,* she dared not to question him. She still had no idea that Brutus was carrying on another secret life.

Three months later an argument occurred between Brutus and Fania concerning Brutus' other woman Gisele. Brutus was not happy by any means. So he arranged for one of his friends to takes him to the mountain at Diquiny, to meet and talk with Fania's parents.

The Deception

Once at Diquiny, Brutus climbed to the mountaintop where the cabin was situated and told Fania's mother to come and get her trash of a daughter and child, as he didn't need any of them in his life.

Brutus then headed back to Port-au-Prince, but deep inside he knew that he had done wrong to his Fania.

One week later, Fania's heartbroken mother arrived in Port-au Prince to get her daughter and grandson and to bring them back home to the mountain at Diquiny.

The poor mother was shocked to see her daughter Fania in such a state of health and mind. Fania had lost weight, was tired and in a state of depression. The mother broke down and cried at the sight of her pathetic daughter.

Once she was back at the mountain with her mother Fania continues breastfeeding her son Sergio. Sergio was not well, had fever and was continuously throwing up. So Fania took Sergio to the general hospital where she was told, *by the doctor,* that for some unknown reason, her son was rejecting her maternal milk.

To find out why this was happening, the doctor did tests on both Fania and Sergio and discovered that she was three months pregnant, which explained, why Sergio was rejecting the maternal milk.

Upon hearing that news, Fania broke down and cried wondering what life had in store for her. She was nineteen years old, alone with a child and a second one now on the way and with no husband to care for them.

Once back at the mountaintop cabin with her son, Fania told her mother the situation and needless to say both the daughter and mother cried out in pain, asking the Lord why was such punishment being placed on their heads?

Tears of Blood

Complete desperation had set in until the neighbor next door, *(a gentleman farmer)*, took pity of Fania's dire situation and helped her by giving her food to eat and this strictly out of generosity with no sexual intent of any sort.

Two months later, Brutus returned to the mountain to take back possession of Fania and Sergio, but finding her there in a pregnant condition, he asked her for an explanation. She replied that; she was already two months pregnant when he had sent her away.

Fania asked him to explain why he had left her and their son in Diquiny without any means of support for clothing and food. She told him that, *had it not been for a gentleman farmed who took pity of them*, they wouldn't have been able to eat properly.

However, she still loved Brutus and accepted to return home with him to see if their relationship could survive the test of time. Brutus didn't say anything and took the pregnant Fania and baby Sergio back with him to Port-au Prince.

Once back home, Brutus found another apartment for Fania and rented the place two streets away from where his other woman Gisele lived.

He then had both of his families living within a few streets of each other, thus making the going back and forth much easier for him.

Once at the new apartment, Brutus told Fania that he thought the baby she was carrying was not his, but that it was the baby of the farmer who had been feeding her and the baby.

Deep inside he knew that he was the father but used the farmer excuse to take away part of his guilt for his unmanly behavior as to how he had treated his Fania.

The Deception

Gisele was told by a friend that Brutus had another woman named Fania living just two streets away, and that she was pregnant and already had a child fathered by Brutus. Gisele realized the situation and not wanting too lose the man that she loved decided not to confront him with the truth, for the time being anyway.

So following the birth of Fania's second child, *a girl named Diane*, Gisele, *wanting to separate Brutus from Fania,* would tell him that there were many men seen visiting Fania at her apartment every time he went to work at the Embassy.

Brutus was quite jealous, and whenever Gisele told him that another man had been seen going to Fania's place, he would have a fit and would go over to Fania's and beat the poor innocent woman who had done no wrong. And this went on regularly, week after week.

By then, Gisele had four children from Brutus and the pressure of all these children were getting to him.

So when poor Fania found herself pregnant with a third child, Brutus accuses her of being unfaithful and claimed that the child was in no way his.

Being furious at Fania over her becoming pregnant with what he believes to be another man's child, he would beat her merciless every week. He told her that he would beat her so bad that the unwanted child would come out of her through her bleeding nose.

He would regularly kick her in the stomach wanting to kill that baby before it was born. At seven months into the pregnancy, Fania realizes that the baby inside of her was not moving anymore and she wanted to go and see a doctor, but Brutus refused any request to see a doctor or to help in bringing that baby to term. He would keep on beating her until the child died.

Tears of Blood

By that time, Sergio, *the first born,* was old enough to understand what his father was doing to his mother but he was too young to be able to intervene. Every time Brutus would start beating Fania, Sergio would run out and sit on the porch floor and would hold his head between his two hands as if to shut out the sounds and screams coming from inside of the house.

He would rock back and forth on the porch holding his head between his hands and crying. Every time his mother screamed he could feel a piecing pain inside of his own heart. Every time he heard the sound made when his father kicked his mother in the stomach, he could feel that same pain in his own stomach and would sometimes throw-up on the porch floor.

Diane the youngest child was much luckier as she was still too young to fully understand what was going on. She would not have much recollection of those terrible days, when her enraged father beat her mother without any justifiable reason.

But for Sergio the story was quite different. Seeing and hearing all of those horrific tortures inflicted on his poor defenseless mother would forever be incrusted in his mind. No child could ever forget the sights and sounds of his helpless mother being beaten and this went on for week after week for several months. Sergio without realizing it would be mentally scarred by those events and this for rest of his life.

One night, towards the end of the seventh month of pregnancy, Fania was having pains in her stomach and she noticed that she was bleeding and that the blood was black instead of being red, so she asked Brutus to please take her to the hospital. Once at the emergency, the doctor discovered that her baby was dead inside of her and that it probably had been dead for a month.

The Deception

The doctor, *using some long pointed instruments*, proceeded to remove what was left of the child piece by piece. The child had been mangled and torn to shreds from all of the kicking that the brutal and merciless Brutus had administered to Fania's stomach during the past seven months.

At one point the doctor shuddered when he removed what seemed to be a piece of the baby's forehead with some hair still attached to it. The child was also enveloped in rotten black blood within the placenta probably caused by the long rotting process that had taken place within Fania's stomach.

The doctor advised that a complete curettage would be necessary for his wife, but Brutus claimed he had no money to pay for it, so he took her home from the hospital without any proper care being given to her.

To insure that the next child was really his and to prevent Fania from leaving for the mountain, *where the farmer was,* Brutus had decided to have intercourse with her immediately and continuously until she was pregnant again.

Shortly following, Fania was pregnant again. But this time, it would prove to be a problem pregnancy.

The lack of adequate treatment and care during her last, *but recent,* pregnancy would surely cause the new fetus to be severally contaminated.

Both Fania and Brutus had no idea whatsoever of what the consequences of such an unhealthy pregnancy would prove to be for the coming child.

With no money forthcoming from Brutus, Fania was not followed by a gynecologist but still carried the baby to its full nine months term. She then gave birth to her third living child, a daughter, and she named her Maria.

Tears of Blood

During the birth process the hospital doctors noticed that Fania's placenta had a smell of rot caused by an infection that was well into an advanced stage. When she had first broken her water, one nurse had even commented on the terrible smell that filled the room.

When baby Maria came, she was fragile and smaller than normal and her skin seemed the color of yellow jaundice, plus the baby showed very little pulse.

The doctors placed the baby in an incubator and advised Fania that they would be keeping the baby for further test. The doctors also advised that they were surprised that baby survived in the first place and only gave the baby a forty percent chance of survival.

They further advised that; if the baby did survive, she would most probably have problems with her sight and hearing, and could possibly be handicapped.

Baby Maria was kept on antibiotics and observation at the hospital for a full month prior to being sent home to her mother.

But once at home, the baby's condition did not improve and she had to be brought to a microbiologist center for further evaluation. The doctors at the center advised, that in order to be able to clean the baby's blood condition, she would have to be fed intravenous with penicillin three times a week and this without fail.

Baby Maria was sent back home and the parents were instructed to bring her to the microbiologist center every Mondays, Wednesdays and Fridays for as long as it takes for the child's blood condition to improve.

The microbiologist had suggested that once the baby was back at home, she should only be cared for by one person, as the child had to be kept free of any infection.

The Deception

Even the chosen caretaker for the child would have to disinfect her hands and wear gloves before touching this baby.

They were warned that should any germ whatsoever enter this child's system, *be it by food or even through her clothing*, it could prove to be fatal for baby Maria.

Brutus realized that Fania, *in her frail condition*, could not possible look after the newborn child and certainly could not be making the trips to the medical center three times week with the baby.

Brutus felt guilty and remorseful of the situation. He knew that Maria was his baby girl, and that the way in which he treated and beat Fania during the previous pregnancy, was in itself the direct cause of the new baby's health condition.

He now believed that possibly, he had miss-judged Fania's faithfulness and in a rare show of human-ship he told Fania that; *from that moment on,* all of the money he got must go for the welfare of his baby girl and that whatever must be done to save that sick child would be done no matter what.

Brutus had even declared to Fania that he would give everything he owned to save his daughter and that they must find someone at once, *to look after Maria on a full time basis,* regardless of what the cost would be.

Fania went to her parents' home at Diquiny and explained what had happened back home,

Then she asked her parents if they would consider letting Julia, *her twelve years old sister,* come to Port-au-Prince to look after Maria.

The parents and Julia all accepted and within a few hours, both sisters were on their way to Port-au-Prince.

Tears of Blood

Maria was a weak baby and she wasn't allowed to drink any maternal milk and only Julia was allowed to have any contact whatsoever with this baby.

At the age of two, *even with all of the penicillin she had been taking,* Maria's skin started deteriorating. Now the baby had big sores appearing all over her body.

Brutus brought her immediately to the microbiology center where the doctors had to increase the doses of penicillin to be taken three times a week. This was now costing Brutus a small fortune, but he borrowed and begged in order to save his precious daughter Maria.

The child's skin condition had become so bad that the slightest touch would cause the skin to peel off. Even to stroke the child's hair would have pieces of hair and skin fall off.

Maria needed special products with a medical base for each and every function required for the care of a baby. She needed medical bandage to clean wounds, and special formulated mils etc... During that hard period of her life, the poor child could not keep anything in her stomach. She vomited and had diarrhea almost every second day during the first three years of her life.

After another year and enormous cost, Maria's skin started growing properly and the miracle baby was back on the road to good health. Maria's recovery had placed great hardship and incurred heavy costs to both Brutus and Fania. At three and a half years of age, Maria looked like a normal child, but the penicillin treatment at lower doses would still go on for another three years.

When Maria was four years old, Fania got pregnant again and nine months later she had her fourth child, a son named Gus. When Gus was born the worse of caring for Maria was over and life got back to normal.

The Deception

During those troubling times, Fania and Brutus had thought that it would have been better to let that sick child die. But after seven years on penicillin, Maria had survived and had become a normal and healthy young girl who no longer needed any special care of any sort.

Fania and Brutus were so happy to have weathered the storm during Maria's sickness and were so proud of their daughter who had never given up against all odds and who grew up to become a beautiful young girl.

Following Gus' birth, money problems started to accumulate. Brutus who had never lived with a budget and to top it all, his gambling addictions started to surface again. The landlord at the apartment complex was fed up with not receiving his rent and he told Brutus to move out.

Brutus knew of a place that was considered a low budget housing section at a less favorable side of town. It was called *(en-bas-Mapou)* which translated to English would mean (under the Mapou tree) and it was by far the worse ghetto in Port-au-Price. This ghetto was a slum where the poorest of the poor lived and no decent Haitians would allow themselves to be seen with anyone from en-bas-Mapou.

In en-bas-Mapou you could find prostitutes, drug addicts, crooks, homosexuals and sick people... You name it and you could find it in en- bas-Mapou.

All the shacks or cabanas, in the ghetto village were situated under a giant Mapou tree. That was why the village became known as en-bas-Mapou.

Those giant Mapou trees were so huge that there could be as many as forty or fifty shacks situated under one tree. The shacks were set in rows of eight or nine with only a sidewalk's width separating the units.

Tears of Blood

From one shack you could see into many others and you could not access the shacks or cabanas by car. You had to leave the car at the ghetto entrance and walk into the complex and this always at your own risk.

This was a destitute place where only the poor and unfortunate lived. This location was actually closer to where Brutus' other wife Gisele lived.

When Fania passed through the gate at en-bas-Mapou, she had shivers run up and down her spine. Fania realized that no one in their right mind would want to live in that God forsaken ghetto. She could not understand why Brutus had decided to send the family there to live.

The first thing they did once they were installed in their new place was to clean up as best they could. Maria was given a broom and told to sweep-up the dirt floor while Diane helped her mother wash the walls to get them as clean as possible.

Sergio sat, *bent over,* on the front porch holding his head between his hands and rocking back and forth the same way he did in the past when he had witnessed his mother being beaten by his father.

Gus stood on the corner of the porch watching what Sergio was doing and couldn't understand why his older brother was carrying on in that peculiar way. Gus had never yet witnessed his mother being beaten by his, *sometimes,* cruel father.

When Maria went into the courtyard to empty the dirt from the bucket she was using, she saw a young boy wearing short pants who was sitting alone in the middle of the courtyard. He was playing a game with some marbles, tossing them inside of a circle he had drawn in the dirt, until one hit the other knocking it out.

Photo from the family archives

Maria's father, Brutus - Photo taken at Port-au-Prince on October 17th 1956 when he worked as a chauffeur for the Liberian Embassy...

Photo from the family archives

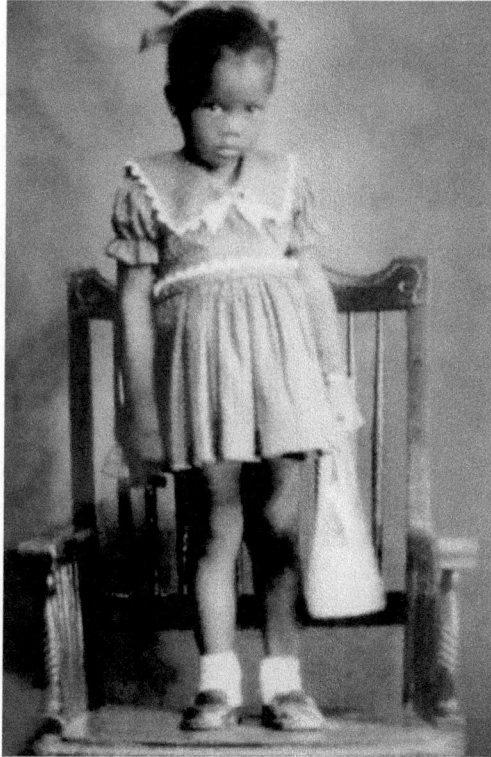

This photo of Maria was taken at Port-au-Prince in 1960 after her skin condition, *as a child*, had cleared up. She was 3 ½ years old at the time of the photo. She kept on being treated with penicillin until she was seven years old and completely healed. She never had any more skin problems from that day on...

– 3 –

Despaired Misery

Fania wondered what was keeping Maria outside so she went out to see and found her daughter talking with the boy that was playing marbles. "What's your name and where do you live?" *Fania asked the boy.*

The boy had answered that his name was Frantz and that he lived just across the courtyard from where they were. He also told Fania that he liked her little girl and wondered if he could play with her from time to time.

Fania told him to go home as she took Maria by the hand and took her inside the cabin. I don't like that boy Fania told Maria and I don't want you playing with him.

One day shortly after, Julia had noticed that Maria's hair and shirt were full of dirt. When Julia asked Maria where all that dirt on her hair came from, Maria had told her that it was Diane who had sprinkled the dirt on her as she often did when they played together.

When confronted with this, Diane would say that she had been simply playing. But Julia soon realized that Diane was jealous of the special attention Maria had received during her sickness. She also learned that Diane was not happy with the birth of Maria, as she wanted to be the only girl in the family.

Tears of Blood

When Julia discussed that situation with Fania, they concluded that there was a possibility that Diane could have been purposely trying to injure Maria, as all in the household knew that Maria had to keep all dirt away from her skin because of the danger any infection could bring upon her. They would watch Diane carefully from that day on as Diane's jealousy of Maria was dangerous.

Two years following Gus' birthday something bizarre had happened to the family. It was raining on that day and Maria had heard strange noises coming from the front porch and she told Julia. When Julia went outside to investigate, she found a baby in a basket that someone had left on the porch. They took that baby inside and saw that it was a boy.

Fania wondered who this mysterious child was and where on earth had he come from? Being there wasn't a welfare system in Haiti to handle a situation where a child is abandoned, Fania decided to keep him for the time being or at least until she could find out who he belonged to.

That evening when Brutus returned home, he asked Fania who that baby was and what he was doing at their home? Fania explained what had happened and asked Brutus what should she do? Brutus answered you picked him up so it's your problem.

With the little money she received from Brutus for the family upkeep, Fania knew that to share the food with an extra child would place a burden on her own children. She had little choice and decided to keep him as one of her own and to share whatever food they had with him.

Three months later, Fania got quite the unexpected surprise when a total stranger came to her front door.

Despaired Misery

The unexpected visitor announced that she was the mother of the boy that had been left in her care. The woman then told Fania, that Brutus was the father of the boy she had left on her porch and that she decided to leave him there because Brutus would not contribute to the support of the child.

When Brutus came home that evening, Fania asked him why he didn't tell her that the child was his. Brutus just told her to shut her mouth and to look after the child. Then; he boldly walked away as if nothing had happened. Fania decided to call the new addition to the family Raymond.

Brutus and Fania would often argue about the boy left on the porch and because of those arguments Brutus' visits became more and more rare. Brutus who used to give Fania one dollar a day to feed the family decided to cut the meager allowance down to seventy-five cents per day, *and to make things worse,* Fania had to continuously send the oldest child to the Embassy to collect the allowance because Brutus had stopped bringing it to her at the ghetto apartment.

Sometimes Sergio would arrive at the Embassy at nine in the morning to collect the money and Brutus would come down and tell him to wait a while and that he would have the money later at eleven instead of nine, but it could be as late as four in the afternoon before Sergio finally got the allowance.

This meant that the family had to wait, *on empty stomachs,* until the end of the day before they could eat and for the children, going without food or milk all day was not a pleasant feeling to endure.

When no money arrived from Brutus, the family had to find other ways to get their needed food for survival.

Tears of Blood

When the money would not arrive and the kids were hungry, Fania would at times send one of the kids to the market place to pick-up whatever scraps no one else wanted, this in order to conjure up some kind of a meal to appease the children's hurting stomachs.

At times Brutus would tell the kid waiting for the allowance that he didn't have it at the moment but that he would come to house at night with some food.

All five hungry mouths would wait until eleven or twelve at night for their father to bring some food. They could not even sleep because of hunger pains they experienced in their empty stomachs.

Finally Brutus would show up empty handed with no food whatsoever to feed the kids and his poor wife that was pregnant again. He had probably lost the allowance at the gaming house playing cards.

Sometimes two full days went by without any food and Brutus would show up empty handed. The hunger for the children was unbearable not to mention the poor pregnant mother. One night they were all so hungry that Gus went out and searched in garbage cans to find bones to bring home so that the gang could pick the bones clean of rotten meat to at least get something into their aching stomachs.

There was a man who worked at the green canopy hospital. He would at times bring the family whatever left over food that had not been eaten by the sick people at the hospital.

All hospital left over food was thrown into large cans for dumping and that is what the family got. They never knew exactly what was in a can or the conditions of how it got there, or what the food had been though before they got it. The mixture of food looked bloody awful...

Despaired Misery

In those cans was food handled by very sick people. Tuberculosis, cholera, all kinds of sicknesses and old people's vomit was thrown in with the leftovers. Only God knew what the family was eating and perhaps it was just as well. But at least it was food regardless of its condition. To a child's hungry stomach, even the worse of food still tasted good.

Several months later, Fania gave birth to her fifth living child. It was a boy and she named him Marc.

Three years went by and then one day, the lady who had left the boy on the porch showed up to take him back. That boy who Fania had cared for and named Raymond would not be seen again for a very long time.

Then a short time later, Fania gave birth to her sixth living child. It was a boy and she named him Joe.

By then Maria was eleven years old and had become close friends with Frantz, *(the boy who was playing marbles in the court yard when she first arrived at en-bas-Mapou).*

They were both the same age and were in the same classroom. They would walk to school together and Maria would often help him with his homework.

The two children would go swimming together and would gather fruits in the forest to eat. They were innocent and had become un-separable friends much to the dislike of Fania, who didn't like Frantz at all.

Fania thought him to be to bold and arrogant and to top it off, Frantz's mother ran a small store from her house just across the courtyard from where they lived.

So Frantz would always be hanging around and watching out for when Maria would leave the cabin so that he could walk and talk with her.

Tears of Blood

Often Fania would tell the young Frantz to go home and to stop bothering Maria. To get around this, Frantz made friends with Gus and would bribe him with some candies so that he could send messages to Maria telling her where they could meet without Fania knowing. This friendship would turn out to be long time lasting.

Continuously looking and begging for food, had sort of become normality for that destitute family. Fania, Julia and the six kids had become so used to going without food that it almost didn't seem to bother them anymore. The misery and pain suffered by the family would also be long time lasting.

One year during summer break Fania had decided to send Maria to her grand mother at Diquini for a holiday. At least there she would have food to eat. Maria was twelve years old and had started her menstrual cycle.

One night the grand mother brought Maria to a voodoo ceremony at the bottom of the mountain. During the ceremony the Unga *(voodoo priest)* cut off the head of a goat and poked its eye out. He then walked over to Maria and told her to eat it.

An Unga likes to drink the fresh blood from a virgin after her first intercourse as this supposedly gives him super powers. When the grand mother saw that the Unga had an eye on Maria, she left the ceremony with Maria at once and made her way back up the mountain to their cabin. That same night arrangements were made to send Maria back home at Port-au-Prince.

It was dangerous for Maria that an Unga wanted her and if the Unga found out where the young virgin was he would come for her and nobody could stop him.

The next morning Maria was on her way back home wondering why the grand mother had sent her back.

Despaired Misery

The following day when Maria got home, Fania explained to her daughter the reason why the grand mother had sent her away. If that Unga had taken her, she would have never been seen again.

One sunny afternoon, Maria was sent to deliver a box of goods to a place where her mother made hats. When she got there with the box she had to deliver, she asked for a glass of water and the lady of the house told her to go and get some in the icebox.

When Maria opened the icebox she saw all kind of food. There were Juices, ham, and meat of all kinds plus small crates of fresh eggs. Maria was hungry and she knew that there were five other kids at home plus her mother and Julia that were also hungry and that there was no food forthcoming.

She couldn't help herself, and she stole eight eggs carefully placing some in her pockets, panties and even inside the home made bra she whore.

When Maria brought the eggs home, Fania asked her were did all of those eggs come from. Maria answered that she stole them for the family. Fania said O.K. I guess we have no choice, as we are all hungry.

That evening all decided to make and have omelets for dinner, but there was a small problem. They had no wood to make a fire plus they also had no oil or butter to fry the eggs with.

However there was an old bottle of (Palma-cristy) oil sitting on a shelf. This was a sort of massage oil used by the Haitians on sore and aching joints. This oil had a foul smell and stunk as of rot. But they had to eat...

So the eldest went outside and gathered pieces of wood and a small fire was started in the cabin, and then, they cooked the eggs with the old massage oil.

Tears of Blood

Fania had Julia and the children sit on the bare floor and form a circle and all were told to hold each other's hands forming a human chain. Then; she placed the cooked omelet in the center of the circle, joined the group within the circle and they all ate the eggs.

The eggs smelled like hell and tasted worse but for hungry children even rot at times tastes good. Fania then lifted her eyes towards the heavens and thanked God for the food they had just received and implored his forgiveness for Maria who had no choice but to steal to feed her destitute family.

During those troubling times Frantz would help as best he could. He and Gus had then become best of friends and he would often have Gus deliver part of his allowance to Maria so that she could get food for the family. During his family dinner, Frantz would secretly place half his diner in a bag and would get that out to Maria so that she had something to eat. Often he would take candies from the store and send then to Maria.

Maria only saw Frantz as a friend but for Frantz it wasn't the same story. He was crazy about Maria.

One week before Christmas, Fania's parents had arrived to spend a week with the grand children before celebrating Christmas Eve in Port-au-Prince with Fania, Julia and the kids. Then the day after Christmas, they were all to leave for a week at Diquiny, to celebrate the New Year with Fania's older sister Rosanna.

Three days before Christmas Fania felt somewhat tired and decided to have nap in the afternoon. She woke up soon after with a splitting headache. So she took some aspirins thinking it was a just normal headache and stayed in bed until seven in the evening, when the headache became a lot more intense.

Despaired Misery

She suddenly felt very weak. Julia, Maria and Sergio were at her side, when; *forty-five minutes later,* Fania lost consciousness. Fania's parents had just walked in.

Clermeli, *Fania's mother,* tried her best to revive her daughter with some traditional medicine and Fania regained consciousness. Julia and Fania's parents didn't find the situation normal and decided that they would take her to the hospital the following morning.

Around eight that same night Fania asked for some tea with a lot of sugar and she drank the tea. Between nine and ten the same evening she fainted again and the mother revived her once more.

As far as everyone was concerned, the situation was not by any means normal. Julia sent someone to find Brutus at the gaming house to tell him that Fania was ill, but he could not be found there at the time.

In the meantime plans were made to take Fania to the hospital at eleven-thirty but she lost consciousness again. This time the mother tried to insert a spoon in Fania's mouth to keep her mouth open so that she could breathe properly. Her mouth was shut so tight that the spoon broke in two. Julia panicked and ran to doctor Westerband's house in the more affluent side of town. She woke the doctor up at around midnight and begged him to come to see her sister who seemed terribly ill and who was fainting continuously.

The doctor's wife pleaded with her husband to do it being Julia helped with all of the sewing in their house. His wife insisted that he should at least go to the ghetto and see what's going on with Julia's sister Fania.

The doctor finally obliged and went to the village ghetto with Julia. When he saw Fania, he looked at Julia and said bring this woman to the hospital at once.

Tears of Blood

As the doctor was leaving in his car, a neighbor, *who was a taxi driver,* arrived and Julia asked him if he could bring her to the hospital with Fania.

Julia, Diane and the taxi driver carried Fania to the taxi and rushed her to the hospital. Before leaving for the hospital, Julia told Sergio to go and find Brutus to let him know what was happening.

Sergio went to Gisele's house and asked a neighbor to go into Gisele's place and to tell Brutus that Fania was very sick and was at the hospital.

The neighbor told Sergio that Brutus was not at home, but that he knew where he was.

Shortly after, the neighbor found Brutus and upon being told that Fania had been hospitalized, he immediately rushed over to the hospital.

Fania's father was sitting on the porch shaking his head from side to side, then; he turned to is wife and said, Fania will not be coming back home.

Maria and the others three kids looked on helplessly and could smell a strange odor in the room. It was as if, *without them knowing it,* they had just smelled the fowl odor of death.

When Fania arrived at the hospital, *around one in the morning,* there was only one doctor available in the emergency to serve the needs of the entire hospital.

Half an hour later the doctor finally saw Fania and said she needs oxygen immediately, but none was available that evening at the hospital.

Fifteen minutes later Fania passed away in the arms of her sister Julia as Diane stood by watching helplessly.

Brutus had just arrived only to find his Fania dead in the arms of her sister Julia.

Despaired Misery

They draped her in white sheets and took her to the morgue. Julia was in a complete state of shock and could not accept having her sister die in her arms and not being able to do anything about it.

Julia and Diane had become hysterical. They were crying and screaming at everyone in the hospital to such a point where the doctor told Brutus to take the women with him and leave the hospital.

Back at the cabin, Maria was standing in front of her window waiting and watching to see if her mother was coming back. Then she saw the three coming home...

Brutus had Julia on one side and Diane on the other and Maria could see that Brutus was holding them up as all three wobbled their way towards the cabin,

At two-thirty in the morning, when Julia entered the cabin, she held up both hand towards the sky. Maria let out a painful cry; she is dead isn't she ...Mother is dead.

Maria shrieked loud enough that the entire family started crying and screaming which in turn woke up the entire village. Neighbors started arriving, asking what's going on... It can't be... We saw her this morning and all was well and so on and so on...

Everyone was in shock and all joined in with the family's pain and all were crying together as if to show unity that night. A bit later Brutus left the premises.

Now someone had to go and tell the bad news to Fania's older sister Rosanna who lived on the mountain in Diquiny.

A young village girl was given the task and at six in the morning she was sent to tell Rosanna that her sister had died and to come immediately to Fania's cabin at en-bas-Mapou.

Tears of Blood

When the messenger knocked on Rosanna's front door, she was asked what she was doing there at that time of the day. The messenger told her that Julia had sent her and that Fania was dead. Rosanna believed that this was only some cruel joke being played on her.

Trying to fool me hey! Rosanna said, as she tore off the messenger's dress. Impossible; this cannot be true because Fania is coming her Saturday to spend New Year with us. But when Rosanna saw the messenger was shaking and crying, she suddenly realized that there was something dreadfully wrong going on here.

She gathered all of her seven children who were still in their pajamas and bare footed they made their way to Fania's house at *en-bas-Mapou.* They had to find out what the hell was going on over there...

A short time later they arrived in the village ghetto and saw that many of the neighbors were crying in front of Fania's cabin. Surrounded by her off-springs, she walked up to the cabin entrance and stood in the doorway with both hands leaning against the door's inner frame.

Then; bending one arm to touch her waist, she shouted to Julia **'Where is my sister?"**

"Fania is at the morgue," *replied Julia,* as she lifted both hands towards the sky in a sign of despair.

"Not true" shouted Rosanna as she pushes her way past every one on her way to the other cabin's room.

She became crazy, pushing people from right to left as she started realizing that maybe her precious sister was really gone. She tore open the second room's door curtain and entered the shabby room, **"No Fania"** she screamed out loud and then she lowered her eyes towards the floor and started to cry.

Despaired Misery

Now there was Julia, Fania's mother and father and the six children, plus Rosanna and her seven children and lot of neighbors, *about thirty people,* crammed into two small rooms in the cabin. All of them were crying tears of blood, *that sad evening,* in the village ghetto of *en-bas-Mapou...*

The next morning, December 24th, Brutus arrived at the cabin and advised that he didn't have enough money to cover all of the cost that would be incurred with the funeral. Being the family had to remove Fania from the hospital morgue and move her to the funeral parlor, Brutus claimed that he had the money to place Fania at the funeral home and to pay for the church service and flowers, but there was no money left to clothe the six children.

Fania had been doing the washing and cleaning for a Mrs. Moore who had a clothing shop situated at the higher class part of the village suburb, so Julia went to see Madame Moore and told her that Fania had died and that she needed help to clothe the six children.

Mrs. Moore was shocked at hearing the terrible news and agreed to dress the kids at her own expense. She made sure all of the six children were properly dressed for the coming funeral service. In the meantime the brothers and sisters of Fania had arrived from Diquiny and preparations were started for the funeral...

On the Eve of the Burial, the 27th of December, there were at least 300 people reunited to pay final respect to Fania. In order to have the traditional wake more money would be needed. All of these people were there to lend support to what was left of the family and to donate as much as they could, which in turn allowed the wake to proceed as expected.

Tears of Blood

Some of them went for water other brought food many helped to serve the mourners and others donated what they could in order to make sure the deceased had a proper and decent memorial service.

The wake was like the end of the world for all of the friends and family of Fania whom was loved by all.

Even Brutus was present for what would prove to be a heartbreaking and unforgettable event for everyone present at the wake. All eyes were focused on the six motherless children and all were wondering what was to happen to these six children with their mother gone.

It was in the afternoon of Dec 28th, the funeral day, and all was ready. The children were all properly dressed thanks to the generosity of Mrs. Moore. The girls were dressed in black dresses and wearing tiny black boot that looked like delicate shoes and they had small hats with a veil covering half the eyes. The boys were dressed in black suits with white shirts and black bow ties.

All had to be at the parlor for 2 O-clock in the afternoon. Julia, *who was then twenty-five years old,* was dressed in black like the two girls and Fania's mother was also dressed in black and wearing a black hat and shoes.

The six children, Julia and Brutus arrived at the parlor in one car and Fania's mother arrived in another car with Fania's two brothers.

The kids hadn't yet realized that they would be seeing their mother for the last time.

The parlor service staff placed the six kids in front of the casket where they saw their mother dressed in a purple dress and with a transparent veil covering her angelic face. The kids stared at their mother in silence.

Despaired Misery

Maria had the impression that her mother was simply sleeping and expected her to wake up and come home with her.

They placed three of the children on one side of the casket and three on the other side with Brutus standing at one end and Julia standing at the other end.

Then; Rosanna, *Fania's sister*, arrived with her brood of seven children and all hell broke lose in the parlor. The place was engulfed with screams and tears of all that were present at that somber affair.

Rosanna walked up to the casket and lifted Fania's veil and shouted ***"where are you going Fania, you leave six children and your going. Answer me Fania, where are you going. You're supposed to be at my place for New Years."***

Poor Rosanna had lost all control of her emotions. She was screaming and crying and turning from left to right and moving back and forth and lifting her eyes and hands towards the heavens as if she was imploring the Lord to wake her out of a terrible dream... But she was not dreaming!

In the corner of the parlor Fania's mother stood in silence as if she was gasping for air. This was caused because the old woman had tied three ropes around her body as if to contain the grief that engulfed her.

One rope was tied at her waist another around her stomach and the last slightly under her breast. These ropes seemed to remove all feeling and pain from within the body.

Suddenly, Ismalie *another one of Fania's sisters,* walked into the parlor. She was also wearing a black dress and high heel shoes. Her wide rimed black hat was slanted on her head as if it was about to fall off.

Tears of Blood

Not being used to high heel shoes, her feet would bend sideways and caused her to walk as if she had been drinking. She walked to the coffin and tore the vale of her dead sister's face and yelled at her. ***"Open your eyes dam you, talk to me, getup, your children need you."*** Then, she tried to lift Fania's body out of the coffin, while saying that she was bringing her sister back home with her and that this was all a mistake.

"No! This cannot be happening, Fania cannot be dead". "I am taking her home with me," she kept on repeating this until the funeral director had no choice but to intervene and tell Brutus, that she had to be removed from the parlor because she was causing a disturbance.

Then the coffin was taken to the church situated in front of the funeral home. Once in the church a choir sang the appropriate hymns and the church ritual was performed followed by tearful eulogies. Then the coffin was placed in the funeral car along with three wreaths of flowers and all made their way to the cemetery.

Brutus was at the church service. But being he was married to another woman, he could not accompany Fania to the cemetery. *Haitian tradition does not allow a man to bury a second wife in a cemetery for as long as his first wife is still living.* That, Haitians believed was a bad omen and would result in misfortune for the man.

The immediate family along with the children walked behind the hearse on foot and behind followed all of the neighbors and friends. It took a good half hour to get to the cemetery and you could hear all of the crying and screaming made by the mourners. The crying was so loud that you could hear the procession of mourners coming from a good block away.

Despaired Misery

When they arrived at the hole in the ground it was hysteria all around. When the coffin was lowered into the ground, Ismalie tried to jump in the hole with Fania's body. It took all of her children's strength to keep her from falling in the hole. Then after everyone threw bits of ground on the coffin all left the cemetery and went on their different ways.

Sergio was close to his mother and when all had left the cemetery, he climbed into the hole and sat on the mother's coffin rocking back and forth holding his head between his two hands. Eventually he returned home.

Later that evening feeling enormous pain Julia and the six children tried their best to comfort each other.

They all gathered together in a circle holding each other and crying as they waited for Brutus to arrive but he didn't show up that evening and eventually they all fell into a deep sleep. The exhaustion and heartbreak suffered over the past week had taken its toll, and one by one they fell into a deep merciful sleep on the dirt floors of their cabin in *en-bas-Mapou.*

The next morning when they woke up they ate some food as there was still quite a bit left over from the wake. They all waited patiently for Brutus to come to the cabin, but they waited till nightfall, and still Brutus had not shown up. Another night held close together and sharing sorrow and pain until all had fallen asleep.

This scenario went on for another three days and now the food was gone and there was nothing left to eat. All of a sudden reality set in and Julia realized that, *possibly;* Brutus had simply abandoned the children leaving them to their own fate. She had a horrible premonition that he would never come back to the cabin or even worse not help the children in any way.

Tears of Blood

The next morning, *Julia who was twenty-five years old at the time,* finding herself with a large family on her hands with no means of supporting them, went out into the ghetto's central courtyard and fell to her knees.

With both arms stretched out and palms facing the sky she cried out in a loud voice. ***"Fannia, Fania why don't you take me with you. What have you done to me, why did you leave us like this - What am I to do with these children?"*** Then she lied face down on the ground sobbing and crying in complete discouragement as the children, *oblivious to what was happening,* watched her from the cabin porch. By then many neighbors had gathered in the yard and watched that dreadful scene helpless to do anything about it.

Julia would send the children each day to find their father at work to see if he would give some money to eat but Brutus kept hiding. Every day Brutus had a different story... He was busy he would come later, or maybe tomorrow. At nights Maria would find her father at the poker tables but he would say he had no money for the family. Sometimes, *as if to cover his guilt*, Brutus would give Maria 2 cents to buy candy...

Finally they all realized that he would not be coming back, nor would he help with the upkeep of the family.

All at once they were each on their own. The eldest were able to find food from friends but the youngest would go without food for days at a time. Julia did some work sewing and by adding pennies she would sometimes be able to accumulate fifty cents or even one dollar and with that dollar at least there was one solid meal every Sunday.

For the next thirteen months they would all discover what the worse kind of abject misery really was...

Despaired Misery

All the children, *including Julia,* had bad periods of frustration and anger and with all of this anger, frustration and misery, the family had become like animals... Six children living in a small two room shack. Four boys, two girls and one adult...

It was as if all lived in a fantasy world where nothing made sense. The children didn't understand where they were or what they were doing in this world. Sometimes they laughed sometimes they cried, and often they couldn't sleep because of hunger pains. All of them were completely distraught.

Julia was surpassed by the events and found herself in charge of six children that had become less than human and completely and totally screwed up.

When she realized the extent of the psychological damage done to the kids, she asked Sergio, *the eldest who was seventeen,* to calm down and to help in supporting the youngest so that all could survive.

There was no more morality in the thinking of these lost children... There followed thirteen months of unmentionable circumstances so horrible that they best not be mentioned.

Sergio was so perplex with losing his mother that all he could do was sit on the front porch rocking back and forth holding his head between his hands.

The kids would separate in the day and each looked for friends in order to eat. Diane, Maria and Gus would hang around with friends in order to find food and the others waited at the cabin hoping the other three would find some food and bring it home... If Maria had a piece of bread left over from begging she would bring it home to share it at night and if no one brought any food at home the youngest, *Joe*, went without.

Tears of Blood

Sergio was the oldest and he had sat so often on the porch floor, *rocking on his bottom*, that eventually one could see his bare butt right through his pants. The death of his mother had not only left him frustrated but he also caused a mean streak to develop in him. At times he would beat up his brothers for no particular reasons.

One day Marc, *who suffered from asthma*, got on his older brother's nerves. Sergio hit him in the chest so hard that, Marc flew against the wall and slid down to the floor while holding his chest and gasping for air.

Maria seeing this believed for a moment that Sergio had killed Marc. When Maria revived him she could help herself and started crying.

The misery inflicted on those helpless children was so unbearable that at times, they thought that they would have all been better off dead.

One afternoon, Gus was over at a friend's house. He had not eaten in two days. He saw his friend eating in front of him, so he grabbed a piece of the friend's bread and took a bite. When the friend's mother saw that, she started slapping Gus in the face until he had spit out that small piece of bread. Then she told Gus to get out and never set foot in their house again. When Gus got home that day he cried until he fell asleep late at night.

On New Year's Eve, Julia wanted to serve the family the traditional Haitian soup. She gave Marc three cents and told him to go to the road merchant and buy a large bone as that would give the potato soup some flavor. Marc saw a suitable bone and asked how much was the bone. The merchant said four cents. Marc knew they needed that bone to make the soup so he placed his three cents on the counter and took the bone away.

Despaired Misery

The merchant cried out "**I said four cents**" and he grabbed the bone from Mark and threw the three cents on the ground. When Marc tried to take back the bone, the merchant took Marc by the neck and beat him until his face was bloody. Marc picked up the three cents and walked home without the bone needed for the soup.

When he got back to the cabin, Julia seeing him with his bloodied face asked him what had happened. When he told her the story, Julia fell to the floor in tears.

There would be no traditional soup for that New Year. When Maria heard the story and saw her young brother's bleeding face, she promised herself that she would do whatever it takes to get her family out of that miserable ghetto that was destroying them.

Maria found a few places where she could get plenty to eat and even bring some extra food home for the youngest, but there were conditions involved for this 13 year old girl, sometimes; rather unpleasant conditions. But the survival of the family merited sacrifices.

Maria was very pretty at 13 years of age and she had started developing a young woman's body. Julia would always sent her to pick up the scraps at the markets as people had pity for the unfortunate Maria and a lot of the merchants would at times give some free food.

But in the cruel ghettos and slums of Haiti, innocent children were given, free candies, food and pieces of needed clothing, but all of those free gifts were not so free. Often the gifts were in exchange for petty sexual favors the older men would expect and demand from young and innocent girls and boys.

Of course the girls and boys caught in this type of vicious activity kept the horrors to themselves.

Tears of Blood

That was the way it was in Haiti in those days and nobody complained or talked about those criminal acts...

But even to this day there are still many countries where that sort of treatment is inflicted on young orphan girls or boys who have the look of innocence on their faces.

One day Julia told Maria to take the fifty cents that she had saved up and to go to the *(trou de sable market)* which means (hole in the sand market), and to gather all that she could so that a warm dinner could be prepared. The *(trou de sable market),* was a beggar's market where past due date and partially rotten food was sold the poor destitute people.

Maria was to get a kind of local potato that was so big it could feed six people and she was to pick up whatever she could find that would help in feeding the hungry gang waiting at home for some food. Maria got things like carrots, vegetables etc...

Maria was also told to get two pieces of specially marinated pork at a cost of two cents a piece. This pork was already unfit for sale to the public, but at this market they mixed a lot of salt with the rancid meat thus killing the smell and making it somewhat acceptable for the poor as eatable meat.

Sergio was sent to pick some broccoli from one of the neighbors' garden, which he did at the risk of having the dogs chase after him. The hungry children sat on the porch with Julia waiting to see what Maria would come home with.

Then, when Maria would arrive with a filled bag hanging over her shoulder she would drop it on the floor in front of the hungry clan and they would tear open the bag to see what bounty had been found.

Despaired Misery

Julia would then have Sergio go outside to get some dry wood for the fire while Maria and Diane were busy chopping the vegetables. Once the fire started in the house a large pot filled with water was brought to a boil, then the cut vegetables and the two pieces of marinated pork were tossed in to the pot. The pork would give this broth a taste of soup and once cooked they would be able to feed their bellies for a good two days.

Sometimes when it had been raining and Sergio got wood for a fire that was still a bit wet, it was Marc who would fan the fire with a piece of cardboard to keep the flame hot enough for cooking.

Maria had a girl friend at school and Maria would often go there after school. The mother of her friend would ask Maria to stay and eat with them. But again nothing was free in Haiti and the girl friend's father would at times ask Maria for oral sex in exchange for taking her with his daughter for ice cream at the soda parlor. Yes, nothing was easy for the poor and destitute in the ghettos of Port-au-Prince if you were helpless and innocent orphan children.

In those days, Haitian men were like a bunch of sick animals who took lusty advantage of helpless women and children. These men acted that way most of their miserable lives so why not take advantage of innocent young girls when they could.

Maybe that was the real reason for the killing of those seven to twelve year old boys at Quanamainte twenty years ago … But at least they spared the children the sacrifice of forcing complete sexual relations for fear of the retaliations that could results from such acts, should a young girl from the ghettos or slums of Port-au-Prince become pregnant.

Yes, they spared that for the girls but masturbation or oral sex... Well now! That was perfectly al right for those perverts and child molesters.

Now, this went on in slums, farms and ghettos but not with the upper class. Those upper class children, were certainly not molested by those perverts... Oh no, that was reserved for the poor and destitute in the slums and ghettos of Haiti.

Yes there were plenty of weird sickos in Haiti, but that problem exists all over the world doesn't it. There should only be one type of punishment applied to those immoral men who like to abuse poor innocent children.

It should be the death penalty and not a nice clean execution but a barbaric one such as slowly roasting their genitals on a fire or even skinning them alive, *like the Indians uses to do,* and maybe even add salt to the wounds and still that would not be punishment enough to make them pay for the hideous acts that they had committed on God's innocent children.

And this misery and degrading pain for Julia and the kids went on for another six months. Yes, seven months of suffering had gone by since Fania had passed away.

Maria learned at an early age what some men are capable of. She had in a way become a woman but she kept secret from Julia what she had to endure so that the family could survive.

One morning after waking up, Maria brushed her teeth and washed herself, as that was the morning ritual imposed by Julia for all the kids. Joe the youngest was yelling that he was hungry. Julia looked at Maria with that, *what will we do look...*

Maria said that she would go out to a friend's place where possibly she could get something for Joe to eat.

Despaired Misery

She went to the girl friend's house and asked her friend's mother if she could spare some food for Joe. The lady gave Maria two oranges that Maria brought home to Joe.

Maria hadn't eaten anything yet and could feel her stomach growling. None of the clan had eaten anything either. Julia was discussing with Maria trying to figure out what they could do to get some food.

Maria said that she had another friend where she might get some food for everyone so she went to the other friend's house but the friend wasn't there and neither was the mother. But her friend's father was there alone. Maria told him that everyone was hungry at the cabin and she wondered if he could spare some food for her family.

Her friend's father said no problem; I can give you some food for your family, but you must do a favor for me. Maria was only thirteen, but she knew what the favor was that the man wanted, so she pleased him and in return he gave her the food to take back to the cabin.

She brought enough food home that day to feed the entire clan. As they were eating, Julia told Maria that she didn't know how Maria could get her friends to keep on giving them food. Maria never told Julia what she had to endure in order to feed the other five kids. Julia pretended not to know, or maybe she didn't want to know what Maria was doing to keep the others eating.

But not all the men were bad in Haiti. There were some who simply felt sorry for Maria and would help out without any conditions or favors in return.

One evening Julia needed rice to make a meal for the clan but she had no money. Maria told her to boil the water and she would get some rice for all to eat.

Tears of Blood

She went to a house where a government man lived to get that much needed rice for Julia but he wasn't home. She kept ringing the bell and noticed that his car was not there so she started to leave.

There was a man watching from the balcony next door and he came down to ask her what she wanted.

She told him the story and he asked why did she need that rice and who was it for? She answered and started to leave when the man went back up the stairs

"Wait a minute," shouted the man, "*I will get you some.*" He came back down the stairs and gave her a full bag of rice asking nothing in return. When she got home with the rice, Julia just shook her head in disbelief and wiped some tears from her eyes.

One night during a bad storm the wind had knocked one of the cabin walls down and the rain was coming inside. Julia wondered how they would repair the wall.

The next morning some of the neighbors got together and put the wall back up. Sometimes people did help out in Haiti, without asking anything in return.

But often, when older men offer to help young girls there are conditions attached to such false generosity. Yes, Maria found out the hard way that many men are sexual predators and often they are the ones you least suspect. Sometimes they are even members of your own family. However that was never the case with her.

One evening, Maria went to visit some friends at a distant village, and around ten that evening, *as she was returning home on a dark and obscure road,* she passed in front of the village church, when; a small white dog suddenly crossed the road in front of her making her jump in fear. She had heard noises behind her and had an ugly feeling that there was something wrong...

Despaired Misery

She felt someone was following her. The dim lights that reflected on the village road seemed a bit brighter and when she turned to look back she noticed that a car was following her on the obscured and darkened road.

Maria was scared and she removed her sandals in order to run. Then she heard the voice of a man in the car. "Where are you going little girl at this time of night?" *said the man*, as he lowered his car's window.

Maria didn't answer as fright had set in and she started walking faster to get away from the stranger.

But as Maria kept on walking, the stranger kept slowly driving alongside her asking, "answer me little girl and don't worry, I don't want to harm you."

"Get in the car, *he said,* and I will drive you home to your parents."... **No**, she cried out... Her eyes had opened wide and her heart began pounding with fear. "My aunt doesn't want me to talk to strangers," *Maria said in a crying voice....*

"Fine then... If you don't want to get in the car, I will follow and protect you until you get home," *the man replied* and he followed her slowly to the ghetto of *en-bas-Mapou.* Then, he parked his car and followed her on foot through the laneways without speaking a word.

When Maria had safely set foot through the cabin door, the stranger was still walking towards the cabin and she could see him approaching the front door.

In her panic, Maria had not had the time to close the door, and suddenly; the stranger was standing in the open doorway and looking inside. The entrance to the cabin was dark as there was no electricity and the oil lamp was at its lowest level in order to save on fuel. It was so dark inside that one could not even identify who or how many people were inside that cabin's room...

– 4 –
Enter the Angel

The stranger stood there in the doorway and it was hard to see his face because of the darkness. It was as if a shadow was standing there.

Julia went to him and asked, "What did this girl do to you" *Maria cried out* "No, No... I didn't do anything wrong. That man followed me home."

"No misses," *answered the stranger,* "she did nothing wrong. I just saw her walking late at night and followed her to make sure she got home safely. This child should not be out late at night without an adult!"

The stranger was still standing in the doorway during this discussion, so Julia primed the oil lamp and told him to come into the house as she set a broken chair for him to sit on. Then, *as best she could,* she explained, *to the stranger,* what the situation was. The stranger identified himself as being Wilner Dorsainville.

While Julia was explaining the whole story to the stranger, the children started arriving one by one and all were surprised to find a stranger in the house. The youngest, Joe, taught he was his father, and he asked Julia if that man was his father? "No he is not your father," *replied Julia.* The stranger was surprised to hear the child asking such a question.

There was a lot of emotion in the room at the time as the kids were surprised to see such a well dressed, gentleman standing in their humble shack. His allure and the scent of his perfume filled the entire room.

Tears of Blood

During the verbal exchange between Julia and the stranger, *Maria stood by the second room door staring at the strange man never daring to utter a single word.*

The stranger, *in turn,* was surprised to see those children appearing out of nowhere one after the other. He was completely shocked when Joe the smallest had appeared naked asking if he was his father. The stranger could not understand what the hell was going on in this place.

The second and third children to appear were Gus and Mark who 'with wide open eyes' kept staring at the stranger's shoes. Then, when Sergio the eldest arrived, wearing torn and tattered pants, the stranger looked to the right then to the left and rolled his eyes upward and just shook his head.

During all of this time, Julia was explaining the entire story to the stranger as to how they all came to be there together, and how they were all starving in her arms and that there was nothing she could do to save them.

Then, the stranger asked. "How many are there in this horrid place?" "Six Sir, Six orphans with no Mother or father sir," *answers Julia,* who started crying as Diane entered the room.

All of this time Maria kept standing in the corner observing the goings on without uttering one word.

Then; that mysterious man pushed up his glasses and looked from side to side looking at everyone one at a time. He glanced at young Maria for a while before looking up and saying, "Pity Lord pity", as Julia swiped her hands looking side to side while gathering the flock together and said, "Here they are the six of them and they have not eaten anything for the past three days.

Enter the angel

"They are all starving in my arms and there is nothing I can do," *she kept repeating,* as she swiped her hands back and forth against each other. Then looking upwards, she kept repeating, "there they are the six of them that Fania has left me with…"

The stranger turned his head and looked at what he believed was another room separated by a doorway with a curtain on a rod acting as a door… "What's in that other room" *he inquired?*

Julia replied, "go and see for yourself and you will understand." He drew the curtain and looked inside and saw some small piles of rags in each corner of the shabby room. Now he understood! *'My god he thought to himself,'* they are all sleeping in this small room with each one having his own place on the dirt floor.

The stranger was out-past by the events. He kept removing his glasses and replacing them sometimes closing his eyes over and over again. He would take deep breaths between these activities. At times repeating "Good lord what is this, how could you allow such misery on these children… Pity Lord, Pity on these poor souls…"

Julia reflected on what was happening and asked herself 'could this be the savior that god has sent onto them to deliver them from the living hell they were in?'

All at once he turned and had a long look at Maria, then he looked at Julia, then he looked at each kid one at a time, and finally he looked back at Julia…Then; stoking under his nose with a bent finger, he turned to Julia and said, "O.K. I want to help you and I will…"

Joe the youngest kept repeating to Julia "I'm hungry" then at that point the stranger took five dollars from his pocket and gave it to Joe. Joe said, thank you.

Tears of Blood

Then Joe ran out of the cabin followed by Gus and Mark. The three hurryingly made their way to Anna's general store that stayed open until midnight.

The stranger turned to Julia and asked, "Do these kids go to school?" "Not since the death of their mother nine months ago." Julia replied, "The eldest boy, what does he do?" "Nothing sir, they all do nothing. They are like animals, cattle waiting to be slaughtered."

"The first thing I want you to do in the morning is to go and buy food for this family as they all must eat." The stranger then said to Julia that he would give her fifty dollars to go shopping and advised her that he would decide what he would do with them the next day.

Wilner Dorsainville was in a state of shock brought on by the events he had just witnessed. He got up and gave Julia the fifty dollars. Julia, *with tears in her eyes,* cried out, "Thank you...thank you... a thousand times thank you kind sir."

"Don't thank me, *he said,* this is but a humanitarian gesture. You are all humans and can't go on like this."

Then he looked at everyone one more time and before leaving, he gently kissed Maria on the forehead and left as mysteriously has he had appeared...

Once the stranger had gone, Joe, Marc and Gus returned to the cabin empty handed. They had bought peanut butter, milk and bread but as the three were starving, they had eaten all of the food before coming back home.

Then, Julia and the kids talked about the strange events that had just happened. Was this a sign of hope for everyone 'Julia pondered. And if that stranger did return, then why and what would he be expecting in return? After all, they didn't even know who he was.

Enter the Angel

All were sitting on the dirt floor when Julia turned to them and said. "There are two things here to consider. First; if he returns it's because God has heard our plight and has sent us a savior, and secondly; if he does not return, we at least have food for the next two weeks…"

Then, they went to sleep happy that night because there seem to be a chance of hope for them, but yet worried, that maybe the kind stranger would not return.

The next morning Julia was up early and she went to the market with the fifty dollars to get everything they needed for the cabin… She bought Flour, rice, beans, oil, charcoal, lamp oil, milk, sugar and soap. In short she bought some of everything in the store, as they had nothing at home in the first place.

She filled two large baskets. The baskets were so large that she had to take a taxi back to the ghetto, as she could never carry all this food herself. The fifty dollars the stranger had given her was a lot of money for their situation they were in and there would still be some money left over after today's shopping.

When Julia arrived with all of those provisions the neighbors were dumbfounded at the site of seeing these misfits of society having so much food all at once.

The six children were waiting on the porch for Julia's return and helped her carry all the goods in… All of a sudden Gus the fourth child started to dance while shouting *"we have food we have food"* as he danced around the baskets of food sitting on the floor.

Then all at once five of the children and Julia made a circle and grabbed Maria and they held her high in the air above their head chanting thank you sister thank you. The room was filled with joy as all kept chanting thank you lord, thank you our dear sister, thank you.

Tears of Blood

Maria was laughing but could not understand what all this commotion was about, but she did enjoy this moment of glory and praise. That Day Julia made a great meal for every one. They ate rice, beans, chicken brew and they could even drink juices and milk. What a day that was. A day none would ever forget.

In this cabin, all took place inside of the four walls well hidden from the nosy neighbors. Close to five in the afternoon, someone knocked at the door.

When Julia opened the door it was the Wilner...

He wore a blue shirt and black trousers and his shoes shined like a mirror... He looked like an Angel standing there, a vision of goodness itself. As he entered, he held in his hands a writing book and a pen.

Julia quickly brought him the only broken chair they had and offered him a glass of juice. "No thank you, *said Wilner,* I don't want any."

Well seated; he opened the writing pad and started with Sergio the eldest. "What does this one do he asked and where is he at with his schooling?" Julia replied that Sergio had completed elementary school but that he had been distressed since the death of his mother. He was seventeen years old and he didn't feel good and seems to be badly traumatized.

Wilner decided that being he had an electronic store, Sergio will take an electronic course and that he would come and work at his store to learn a trade...

As for the second oldest child, Diane, what did that one do, he asked Julia? She is just as traumatized as Sergio by the death of the mother. She is 16 and is still in elementary school but she likes sewing... So, Wilner decided for her to continue school and later she will go to a sewing house to learn the trade of seamstress...

Enter the Angel

Now it was Maria's turn... What does this one do and what are her problems? Julia replies that Maria is very intelligent and that she is 13 years old and has almost finished her primary schooling but that since the death of her mother, Maria doesn't listen to me and is always outside walking the streets seeking friends...

"Her I will take to my charge personally. First thing; she must have proper clothing and decent shoes. She must always be well dressed, clean and with her hair properly groomed. She must be limited to school and home... No question here of this child being out on the streets alone again! Am I making myself clear on this?"

"I understand Monsieur", *replied Julia*. Julia quickly realized that her first and most important task would be making sure that Wilner's orders, *concerning Maria*, were followed to the letter.

For the three youngest, Gus, Marc and Joe, there was no question here. They would go to school...

"From now on, Maria will attend a private school," *advised Wilner*, "and tomorrow, I will have a small bed brought over for her to sleep on."

Julia certainly did not want to jeopardize the aid this stranger would be bringing to this poor and distraught family. So she would obey his orders without question.

Julia's functions from then on would be to supervise the upbringing and behavior of all the six children and the application of Wilner's directives to all of them.

It was obvious that Wilner was an organized man who would not tolerate any disobedience to his running of that dysfunctional and pathetic family. "That cleared the problems of the children's duties and obligations, *said Wilner,* now we will look at the housing situation..."

Tears of blood

Wilner would take care of the families' needs. Food and clothing would be provided and private school fees for Maria. Everyone would be supplied uniforms, books and pencils.

Following the initial set up for everyone, Wilner had electricity installed in the house so that Maria could do her homework at nights.

One evening, *soon after,* Wilner told Julia to have Maria ready in the morning, as he would be taking her to town with him.

That evening before bed, Julia talked with Maria and told her that she would be going into town with Wilner in the morning and that she must obey whatever the man tells her to do being the family's welfare was now in her hands. Maria was an innocent child and she was scared but understood what Julia meant.

The next morning, Julia had Maria wash herself twice to make sure that the thirteen year old girl was clean and fresh everywhere.

When Wilner arrived, Maria was very nervous not knowing what to expect or what lied in store for her. He told Maria to get in the car and they drove to town.

Maria sat close to the door with her hands grasped together as if she was in prayer, when Wilner, *seeing she was nervous,* told her to relax and enjoy the car ride into town. Once in town the first thing Wilner did was to take Maria to eat in a restaurant.

After dinner he took her to a store and bought her some shirts, sweaters, shorts, and dresses. Some under clothes and her first wrist watch. When they got back in the car Maria couldn't believe all that he had bought for her. She looked at him in abandonment and asked him where he was taking her. He smiled and said home.

Enter the Angel

When they arrived at the cabin, Julia was amazed to see all the clothing that Wilner had gotten for Maria.

Once Wilner had left, Julia looked into Maria's eyes and asked her what had happened in town with Wilner?

Nothing replied Maria, we ate at a restaurant then we went shopping and he brought me home.

Hearing that answer from Maria brought tears to Julia eyes. She had expected the worse scenario for this thirteen years old girl. They both cried as they hugged each other, but those were tears of joy and not pain.

Wilner use to come and visit at least 4 times a week to make sure all was running as to his plan. He brought the entire family to the cinema and to the Champ de Mars for ice cream. All these trips were in his truck.

Wilner looked after Maria as if she was his own daughter. At every visit he made to the cabin, he would look over her school homework and would sign the sheets. Then she would need to return signed sheets to the teacher at the private school. He personally knew the teacher and had her reporting on Maria's behavior.

Wilner often asked Maria if she had any experiences such as kissing or playing with young boys to which Maria always answered that she had had none as she knew that was the answer that he wanted to hear.

She never dared tell Wilner of the abuse she had endured with the older men before he took over the bringing up of the six kids. She would keep that terrible secret hidden for many years to come in her life.

One day, *realizing that all of the six kids were traumatized with the death of their mother and the desertion of their father,* Wilner decided to take the six kids to a psychiatrist for proper evaluation.

Tears of Blood

To all the questions asked by the doctor, the kids would only reply that they didn't know or they would simply stare at the doctor and say nothing.

When asked if they missed their mother, the kids answered yes. When asked how they felt about the loss of their mother, the kids would again answer that they didn't know. The doctor could not get the kids to open up in any way whatsoever.

The doctor then asked Wilner to step into another room to talk with him privately. He advised Wilner that all of the six kids were sick and traumatized at many levels. To treat all of the six children would be a long process and would prove to be rather costly.

If the kids survived trough that ordeal they would keep sequels to their mental health for all of their lives. Wilner wanted to have Maria treated alone but she refused saying it would have to be all of them or none. They left in Wilner's truck and went home.

This went on for two solid years, *with Wilner looking after everyone as best he could,* until Maria was 15 years old...

Maria had turned into a beautiful young girl and started asking herself why Wilner took such special care of her and why was she the only one to go to a private school? How come she was always well dressed and pampered by everyone in the family?

One day Maria asked Wilner why he took her and the family under his wing and if he considered her as his child, or; was he preparing her for something else?

Wilner just lifted his head upwards, stoked his nose as he usually did, adjusted his glasses, grunted a few times and smiled without saying a word.

Enter the Angel

Then one day, late afternoon, Maria was talking to a cute seventeen years old boy on the corner of the street when Wilner arrived in his car for the usual visit.

He walked by Maria saying hi as he passed by her but three or four steps later, he turned to Maria and told her get herself home right away...

Maria ignored him and kept talking to the boy. Then Wilner came back and stepped between the two and he slapped her twice in the face.

Then Maria and Wilner both entered the cabin. Maria was crying and she asked Julia what's going on here.

Am I being used as a hostage to the betterment of the family? Why did this man strike me? Of what right does he have to strike me? He is not my father, so why must I obey everything that he orders me to do, and why is it only me being treated that way?

Julia answered that she only did what Wilner told her to do and that they all must do the same...

Maria answered that she was an orphan and didn't have to obey anyone's orders... From then on she would do whatever she wanted and with anyone she pleased.

Wilner told Julia, that; if she can't control Maria and if Maria does not obey his orders, then all of the family will pay for her rebellious behavior.

Maria was now 15 years old and all her pieces were in the right places. She was now a young woman and the boys excited her quite a bit, specially the boys from the upper class of Port-au-Prince.

In the past Julia began looking everywhere for Maria at four in the afternoon in order to get her home by five so that Wilner would find her home when he visited.

Tears of Blood

Now things had changed... Maria only came home when she pleased and at the time she pleased. She did no more home work for the private school. She had become a rebel teenager as most kids are at that age.

When Maria would misbehave, *as to Wilner's liking,* he would grab her by the shoulders and shake her vigorously while giving her hell. These shaking sessions were worse when it had to do with teenage boys being involved with Maria.

Maria realized that Wilner was at times behaving like a jealous boyfriend and yet he had never approached her in that sort of a way. He had never told Maria that he was considering her as anything else but a daughter.

One day Maria and some of the other girls from the village decided to go to a weekend beach party and she stayed away from home for the weekend. When she got home, Julia told her to get out and find somewhere else to stay.

Maria said fine and she started gathering her clothes but when Julia saw that Maria would leave, she had a change of heart and asked Maria to forget what she had said and to please stay with them at the cabin.

Maria's crisis lasted a good six months... No more home work, coming home late and at times not coming home until the next day ...

Following Maria's rebellion, the other children being grown up followed her lead and all the six kids had now become rebellious in turn. Julia had completely lost the control over everyone...

Even though Maria had become uncontrollable and the other kids no longer paid respect to Wilner, he kept coming to visit every third day and kept on giving the necessary money to support everyone.

Enter the Angel

Sergio was now busy working at Wilner's business improving his electronic skills, but he would take fits against every one in the store. He had no respect for anyone and he kept up his bad habit of scratching his butt in front of everyone...

One day, *for no reason at all,* Sergio told Wilner's wife that she had lost her husband to another woman a long time ago and that his young sister had taken him and that was why he was there working in the store.

He told her that his sister Maria was her husband's mistress and that her husband was going to leave her because of her age and that compared to his beautiful young sister, she had nothing left to offer her husband.

Being terribly upset with what had just happened Wilner's wife went to him and asked what Sergio was talking about. Wilner answered that Sergio was a mentally sick boy and that he would talk to him about his foolish behavior and that it would not happen again.

Wilner's wife was furious and told her husband that she didn't want to see that man in the store any more.

That evening Wilner came to the house to talk with Sergio... "Why did you go and tell my wife all of those stories?" He asked... Sergio told him that he was a charlatan and that he didn't even know anything about electronics. It's your employees and not you that know the business and you are making money off their skills.

Sergio went on to tell Wilner that he used people for his own benefit and that he didn't really care for anyone but himself.

Wilner answered; "If that was the case then you're fired... Don't set foot in the store again." Sergio was twenty years old at that time and never realized the damage that his behavior had caused to his family.

Tears of Blood

A few days later Maria got a strange message from Wilner's wife. The message came by the bias of an influential person in the government. It threatened Maria, telling her that if she didn't leave Wilner alone, she would disappear never to be found again...

Maria went to Julia and informed her of this strange message. Julia said that she would discuss the situation with Wilner. When Wilner came the next night and when Julia informed him of the message, he replied that it was only small talk and that it was not serious and nothing to be worried about.

A few days later Wilner came back and told Julia that the messages from his wife were serious indeed and that his wife was contemplating getting rid of Maria. So that, *from that moment on,* they must be extra careful, as his wife was having him watched...

From that day on, the visits dropped drastically to visits as few as once a week and being that Maria was always gone, she didn't see much of Wilner anymore...

At the end of the schooling year Maria got her diploma and decided not to return to school. She had figured that Wilner kept giving Julia money anyway and that there would always be food on the table.

Wilner's visits became less frequent and he was not paying for Maria's schooling anymore since she had told him of her decision to abandon her studies.

Maria was sixteen by then and had developed into a beautiful, full-bodied young lady. She had become a rebellious teenager and her attentions had starting centering on the handsome young men that were always waiting for a chance to win her favors.

Her outlook on men's behavior had begun taking a different direction. She now saw men in a different way.

Enter the Angel

She started understanding that there was quite a difference between dirty old men taking advantage of innocent young girls in obscure places and older boys who were interested in open relationships.

Young men with ages ranging between eighteen and twenty-five were much more fun to be with. They could go out dancing, go to movies, swimming and partying at the beaches and so forth. She would even be invited to meet with some of the young men's parents.

For Maria, the next two years would prove to be a time of discovery as to who she was and what she could do as a teenager approaching adulthood...

– 5 –
The Rebellion

Maria had become close friends with eight other girls from the ghetto and all of them were exceptionally good looking. All of them including Maria had become boy crazy as most teenage girls tend to do at sixteen.

These girls were all Créole and the boys from the upper class of Port-au-Prince would swarm to En-bas-Mapou for a chance to be with some of these girls as Créole girl were reputed to be the best looking girls in all of Haiti.

Also the boys from the upper class of Port-au-Prince knew that the girls from the ghetto were quite good at petty love making as they had experience brought on by the treatment they endured from older men in order to survive the harsh life of being poor girls in Haiti.

This made for a situation were both the boys and girls could exchange moderate sexual pleasures without risking any unwanted pregnancies as no boy from the upper class would dare impregnate a low class girl from En-bas-Mapou. Complete sexual relations between those two classes of teens were out of the question.

Every weekend the upper class teenage boys would drive to the ghetto in their parent's cars and pick up the girls and take them to the beaches and clubs were they could party. Then, they would drive the girls to secluded places were the petty lovemaking would take place.

Tears of Blood

One day Maria met a boy who was studying to be a doctor. His name was Clifford and the two became quite serious about each other and Clifford didn't care about where Maria came from and he didn't see the difference between classes of people in Haiti.

There was a party being held at Clifford's parent's home and he decided to invite Maria to the party. He took her shopping and got her a beautiful dress and shoes and a matching purse.

Then the night of the party, Clifford made sure not to hold Maria to close when they danced together as the parents were scrutinizing every move that Maria made.

Maria noticed that the parents would glance at each other, as they commented, on the good looking couple, their son and Maria projected to be. After the party the parents showed approval of their son's choice and Maria was invited to have diner with them the following week.

When Clifford drove her home that evening, Maria was the happiest she had ever been in her life. The thought of having Clifford, *a doctor,* as her potential husband brought tears of joy to her eyes. Clifford also had serious thoughts regarding their relationship as he had fallen deeply in love with Maria.

Three days later, Clifford met with Maria and gave her some terrible news. It seemed that his mother had had a detective check out Maria and the fact she was an orphan from En-bas-Mapou was discovered and brought to her attention.

She apparently was furious at her son for having brought a low class girl to the party they hosted in front of family and friends. Clifford was instructed to never see Maria again and furthermore to make sure of this the mother decide to send him away to study in the US.

The Rebellion

The two sweethearts held each other close and cried as they both knew that nothing on earth would change the outcome of their dire and doomed relationship.

Clifford could not throw away his life for Maria and she didn't expect or asked him to consider that option either. She would never see Clifford again.

Maria was devastated by that unexpected turn of events and she started believing that maybe she was no better than a low classed poor girl from the ghettos of Haiti and that she would remain that way for the rest of her life.

But she had been through so much hell in her young life that she decided not give up. She believed that one day, *somewhere,* things would change for the better.

Maria's other seven girl friends also discovered that although they met many of Port-au-Prince most eligible bachelors, no serious relationship, *passing petty love making,* could be expected for the girls. All they could expect from the upper class boys were occasional gifts, entertainment, petty lovemaking, and nothing more.

This discovery by the girls brought on a defensive attitude on their part. They would intimidate and threaten any girls from outside of En-ba-Mapou that would dared mingle or interfere with any of the relationship the ghetto girls would be contemplating with young men.

They formed a fraternity and called themselves the gang of eights. Girls from outside of the close fraternity soon found out that you didn't play around with any of the boys that belonged to a girl from the gang of eight.

The gang of eight would at times go to neighboring villages to intimidate and even beat up any unwelcomed competition. Girls from other villages stayed away...

Tears of Blood

It was time for the annual carnival in Port-au-Prince and the government festivity organizers had to select three young girls to participate in the general parade that would pass in front of the president review stand.

Having heard that there were some beautiful and sexy Créole teenage girls in En-ba-Mapou, organizers came one day to select candidates for the parade and the beauty contest to select the Queen on the carnival.

Maria was the ringleader of the gang and she along with two others were selected and instructed to go to Port-au-Prince for instructions and to be fitted with the costumes they would wear on the Presidential float in the parade.

On Haiti's national holiday, the carnival parade was to pass in the streets of Haiti and wind its way in front of the presidential palace were the President himself would be amongst the dignitaries who would review and by the same token elect the carnival Queen.

The girls costumes consisted of a mesh see through dress covered with flowers and green leaves. The would have to be half naked under the dress and when the presidential float would arrive in front of the review stand, the three girls were to tear open their dresses thus exposing their naked breast to the president and dignitaries. These would then select which one of the girls would be crowned as carnival queen.

Maria won the contest and was crowned Queen of the carnival and she was awarded the five hundred dollar prize that came with the title.

Being she was only sixteen years old, Brutus, *being her father,* claimed the prize in Maria's name. He told her the money would go towards buying her clothes and things, but he spent it instead on gambling and drinking

The Rebellion

The five hundred dollars in prize money was a lot of money in those days and Maria never saw a cent of that prize money. But there were other unexpected benefits that came with the contest for all of the gang of eight.

Now, instead of only having the upper class boys hanging around with them, government officials were now part of the men that visited En-ba-Mapou seeking the company of the Créole girls. That gave the girls openings to be with the higher echelons of the Haitian Hierarchy thus leading to better gifts and services in exchange for petty sexual encounters and that, always without the risk of unwanted pregnancies.

That would prove important for Maria in the future as she knew well that survival for a poor girl in Haiti depended a lot on who you knew and the more important they were the better it could serve you.

Then one day Wilner told Julia that his goal was to push Maria to her limits to make sure she had proper schooling and a trade, *but being she quit,* he therefore had to quit also and leave then all to their own fate...

Wilner was complete demolished and deceived at the turn of events when all he did was try his utmost to save a miserable bunch of children from a terrible fate...

Wilner was now having serious problems with his own wife at home all caused by Sergio's un-thought of and foolish remarks.

Either way, it was Maria who brought him to *(en bas Mapou)* and it was her own behavior that destroyed what Wilner was trying to do.

Before leaving for good, *when Maria was seventeen,* Wilner had told her that if she ever needed anything or was in any kind of trouble in the future to let him know.

Tears of Blood

If she could not get to see him, she could contact his friend Dubiton, who would get the message to him and then, he would take care of her problem.

When Wilner had presented Maria to this so called government big shot friend, *a Colonel Dubiton,* the man instantly fell in love with Maria and this in turn would lead to a future relationship. It turned out that Dubiton was never a Colonel in the military. He wore a military uniform but was really a member of parliament.

One day Maria got a message from Dubiton, saying that Wilner had a message for her. When she got to his office, there was no message for her from Wilner... It was Dubiton who wanted to see her.

Once in the office he started kissing Maria and said that he wanted a serious relationship with her, so they agreed to meet the next day.

The next day he took her to a strange motel where you exited from the other side of where you entered and told her that he wanted to have sex with her. Maria told him no being she was still a virgin...

Dubiton laugh and told her, *that being she was Wilner's mistress,* how could she claim to be a virgin?

Then Maria explained the situation to which Dubiton asked if he could verify if she in fact was still a virgin Maria agreed and with his finger he tested her and found that indeed she was still a virgin.

So they had a relationship based on oral sex and masturbation while keeping her virginity throughout that somewhat serious relationship. He was waiting for the right moment to take her. One day after staying with him all day in a hotel, she realized that she had to get away from Haity before it killed her. She told him that she wanted to go away... Where to he asked her?

The Rebellion

Canada she replied. No he said, you will stay here with me, but if you want I will give your older sister Diane an exit visa for Canada.

That night, *back at the cabin without Julia knowing anything of what was going on,* Maria told Diane that she could get her a visa to go to Canada.

A few days later Marie took Diane to Dubiton's office and he called the Canadian embassy and arrangements were made. Three months later Diane left for Canada...

She would be the first of the six children to leave the hellhole of Haiti for a better world. One of the conditions that Maria gave her own exit papers to Diane was that; once installed in Canada, Diane would bring the two youngest Marc and Joe to Canada.

Once Diane gone, the relationship between Dubiton and Marie became more and more intense. He wanted to take her but she was scared and refused and eventually, she terminated all relationship with Dubiton.

Then one day Wilner was made aware of the goings on between Dubiton and Maria. Upon finding that out he terminated all communication with Julia and Maria.

That would have been another mistake on Wilner's part. He should have talked to Maria to find out exactly what had been going on between her and Dubiton.

Years later someone told Maria that Wilner had confided that he had experienced great sadness when they separated because he was waiting for her to grow up and that he planned to divorce his wife and marry Maria.

Maria upon hearing this wondered why Wilner had never told her of his intentions, as she would have waited for him. But fate had decided otherwise.

Tears of Blood

Then there followed months of partying and beach parties for the gang of eight, until one day when Maria was introduced to a musician named Lapierre. That meeting would change Maria's outlook on life in a way that no one could have imagined.

Lapierre played the guitar in a popular group that played the Port-au-Prince dance circuit. He and Maria soon became close friends and eventually sweethearts.

Lapierre was an imposing figure of a man with all of a musician's bad habits, which included heavy drinking. But Maria felt secure and protected in that man's arm regardless of her man's faults.

It got to the point where the two were inseparable and Lapierre would refuse to play with the band unless Maria was in the audience. Often the other band members would chase all over town to find Maria to bring her to the club they were playing so that Lapierre would play music with them.

Maria had finally found a man who cared for her and with the growing relationship she began to see herself with the possibility of having her own family, a real family with a father, mother and children.

One thing that worried her was that Lapierre would often drink while driving. She tried her best to convince him to refrain from drinking while he drove but to no avail. She loved him unconditionally so she accepted the faults that come with any relationship.

Then one cool evening, *Valentine day 1975,* Lapierre took Maria to their favorite parking place for some petty lovemaking. They had both been drinking and Maria was at the peak of her ovulation cycle. They got carried away in the heat of things and she gave her virginity to the man who was to become her future husband...

The Rebellion

Because of Maria's knowledge when it came to petty love making, Lapierre had always believed that Maria was by no means a virgin. In the past months when he tried to have sexual intercourse with her, she would refuse over and over again telling him that she was a virgin but he believed she was just playing hard to get.

When he took her that first time and saw how she screamed with pain while being taken by him and then seeing all the blood that covered the back seat of his car he realized that she had been telling the truth all along.

That night they held each other close and cried together when he assured her that they will be married together and form the family she so dearly desired.

One month went by and Maria didn't get her period, then a second month and still no period. He would ask about it every day and they came to the conclusion that quite possibly Maria was pregnant.

In order to care for his soon to be wife and child, he got a spare time job driving a truck delivering goods between Port-au-Prince and the Dominican Republic.

When Maria was three months pregnant, Julia was preparing to leave Haiti for Canada to join her future husband, a man that she had known since she was twelve. Maria never told Julia of her condition fearing that Julia would have postponed her exit out of Haiti towards her new life with her man in Canada.

Maria also hid the fact that she was pregnant from everyone except Lapierre. Maria had what one could call a baby face. Even at eighteen years of age, most who didn't know her personally would have only given her fourteen or fifteen years of age. During her fourth month of pregnancy, Maria started showing a belly...

Tears of Blood

Her friends were in total shock when they saw that she was indeed pregnant. Who did this to you some would ask? Who raped you others inquired? It had become the talk of the village when people saw such a young looking girl in a pregnant condition.

When Lapierre informed his family of the situation, his parents told him that the coming child must be someone else's as Maria did have a reputation and no one would have believed that she had remained a virgin throughout all of her eighteen years.

Lapierre was furious at his family. He let them know in no certain way that it was he who had taken Maria's virginity and that it was he who was the father of the baby that Maria was carrying and further more that he was going to marry her.

Lapierre's told his parents that if they didn't accept Maria as his wife, then; they no longer had a son. Being that he was the only son they had, the parents had no choice but to accept the situation and this regardless of any past opinions they may have had about Maria's relationship with their son.

Maria and her husband to be had discussions as to how he would provide for the upkeep of the new family. A musician in a small band certainly would not make enough money to properly look after a family.

Lapierre decided that he would take the regular full time job of driving the fruit delivery truck between Port-au-Prince and the Dominican Republic.

Maria accepted the decision of her man but worried about his drinking habit when he drove. She implored him not to drink while driving the delivery truck. He promised that he would not drink while driving anymore being that he would soon have a family to look after...

- 6 -

The Final Escape

The next two months proved to be difficult for Maria. Being pregnant meant no more hanging out with the gang of eight. No more beach parties and dancing. All of a sudden reality had set in when she realized those days of fun and rebellion, were over. Now life had taken on a different direction and she would have to prepare for the new style of living that awaited her.

But in a way she was happy and content. She would finally have her own real family with the first man she ever loved. Their love was mutual and they both planned on having a large family and a comfortable home together.

Her husband to be was a big, strong man. He was stubborn, but when he put his mind to doing something nothing could stop him. In Maria's eyes the future looked good and she had finally escaped the hell she had lived through for so many years.

She got used to the villagers talking about her and staring at her when she walked by and it no longer bothered her anymore.

At five months pregnant and with both Julia and her sister Diane gone to Canada, Maria found herself alone and looking after her four brothers still with her in the cabin. This was taking its toll on her and it reminded her in a way, of her own mother's previous dilemma.

Tears of Blood

One Day, *Frantz her childhood friend,* came to her and told that her he didn't believe it when he had heard that she was pregnant. He stared at her swollen belly then he turned and ran away. Maria had noticed that he had tears in his eyes when he had observed her belly.

The next day a girl friend had told her that Frantz had cried all night when he saw her in the state that she was in. She realized then that the friendship she had had with Frantz since they were twelve had evolved into something serious for him.

During the past two years, Frantz had tried to get close to her, but Maria found him to be much too young when compared to the older and more mature men that she had been dating. Even though Frantz had become close friends with her four brothers, Maria never gave him any serious though or time of day.

Four months later, *while her husband was out of town on a fruit delivery,* Maria gave birth to her first child, *a daughter named Sabrina.* But on that very day fate would give her another disastrous blow.

The delivery was extremely painful, as the baby was placed in a feet first position. It had to be delivered by Cesarean and this without any available anesthetics.

The nurses wanted to stitch her up without using any anesthetics but a doctor told them to wait until morning when a supply of anesthetics was expected.

Maria was then placed in a shared bed inside one of the general hospital rooms for the night with nothing but a towel between her legs to control the bleeding and to prevent any infection from entering her body.

At nine that evening, Gus and Marc visited Maria in her hospital room and brought her some fruits and fish to eat. They stayed there comforting her until morning.

The Final Escape

In the morning when the anesthetic finally arrived, a doctor stitched her up and after the nurse had cleaned her up, she was sent home with her baby.

The hospital room she was in had many beds and there were two women per bed. Each woman slept at their respective end of the bed with their heads being next to the other woman's feet.

When Maria left the room with her baby she was wearing a white shirt and a short blue skirt. Her nipples were leaking milk so she had placed two face towels over her breasts to prevent her shirt from being wetted by the breast milk.

When she left the hospital room, she was carrying her small baby that had been wrapped in a white towel and as she left the hospital room, she glanced at a mirror at the end of the hallway and saw her own reflection.

She looked like a young teenager that was carrying her little sister and not like a mother who had given birth to a child. When she walked past other people in the hospital, some shook their heads in disbelief for Maria had a baby face and looked no older than fifteen.

Maria's husband never showed up at the hospital to bring her home, because; *earlier that day,* he had been killed in a trucking accident in the Dominican Republic.

It seemed that on his way to deliver a truckload of fresh fruits to the Dominican Republic, Lapierre had consumed too much alcohol and fell asleep. His truck overturned and fell into a ravine killing him instantly.

She was devastated upon hearing that horrible news and as she cried for the loss of her man whom she loved dearly, she cursed him at the same time.

Tears of Blood

"How could you drink and drive your truck while knowing you had a woman and a coming child waiting for you to come home to," *she kept on repeating.* Her four brothers looked on helplessly and were unable to do or say anything to ease her pain.

Maria was without a husband, an un-experienced mother with a newborn on her hands, and with four brothers to look after. The new life she had dreamed about had just crumbled apart before her very eyes.

The life of hardship she had endured for such a long time was in no way over. It would seem that all of the abject misery, *that life could deliver,* would keep on haunting her forever...

When Maria arrived home with the baby, she had no idea of what to do or how to care for the child. She was totally discouraged until a Madame Estache, *a dear old friend of Fania,* offered to help Maria and instruct her on the caring and upkeep of a new born baby.

She was dead tired from the childbirth ordeal and could not get any sleep because Sabrina kept crying all of the time always wanting to find her mother's breast.

The next morning Maria knew that she had a dilemma on her hands. She knew that a man's help was needed to enable her to properly care for her daughter and four brothers.

Being dead tied and sore from the childbirth, she certainly didn't want a man around who would be trying to sleep with her all of the time. Haitian men didn't care about a woman's condition of feelings, so finding the proper person to help could prove to be difficult indeed.

She remembered one young man, a taxi driver named Ti-Co that seemed gentle and understanding. He had shown interest in her over the past two years.

The Final Escape

However, she never paid much attention to him being he was young and a short man. Maria liked the older and bigger guys. Nonetheless, she had someone contact Ti-Co to tell him that she wanted to see him.

The same day Ti-Co arrived at the cabin to speak with Maria. She explained to him the situation she was in and how the death of Lapierre had left her with a newborn baby girl, penniless and without anyone that she could to turn to for help.

Ti-Co told her that he would help with the feeding and upkeep of the family and that she should not worry as he understood the condition that she was in and he would not attempt to bother her for the time being.

Ti-Co went to the general market and purchased all of what was needed to take care of the family and the baby girl. When he came back, he had brought food, milk, soap, oil and diapers for Sabrina.

When times were tough, Maria had sold the wooden bed Wilner Dorsainville had bought her and instead had taken an old metal bed from a friend to sleep on. But that rusty old bed was noisy and Ti-Co found it to be improper for her and the baby to sleep on, so the next day he had a solid wooden bed delivered to the cabin.

During the next three months, Ti-Co took care of everything. But those months proved to be troubling times for Maria. The parents of Lapierre wanted to take Sabrina and bring the child up as one of their own.

Maria had made it clear that she would not let go of her daughter whatever the cost. She wanted and loved that daughter more than anything else in the world and no one could change her mind.

One day when Maria came home from the market, she discovered that Sabrina was nowhere to be found.

Tears of Blood

Upon inquiring of the whereabouts of Sabrina, Gus had told her that Lapierre's parents came and took her away to their home. The family had decided that; *being Lapierre was the only son in the family,* his daughter was rightfully theirs.

Maria went immediately to the parent's home and took Sabrina back with her to En-bas-Mapou. She made it clear to Lapierre's parents, that to take Sabrina away from her could only be done over her dead body.

The Lapierres eventually gave up trying to claim their son's daughter and the relationship between Maria and Sabrina's grand parents deteriorated to the point where they no longer existed. There would be hell to pay for anyone who tried taking Maria's child from her.

Maria having a child and four brothers to look after and without a husband bringing home the money to feed the lot caused a severe problem. That brought back the memory of the hardships suffered when her mother died and Maria would not accept that type of survival again so she made a decision to bring a man into the house that would provide, as a husband should.

Ti-Co had offered to move in with her and help in the support of the family on a regular basis but Maria was still not ready for a live-in relationship with any man and specially with a man she really didn't care for.

Six months went by and there appeared another candidate who was in love with Maria. It was Frantz her childhood friend. He was the same age as Maria but he was still studying as his parents could afford sending him to school. He was the same age as Maria and taller than the taxi driver and was jealous of seeing Ti-Co around Maria. Frantz was not only of a jealous nature. He was aggressive and possessed a nasty mean streak.

The Final Escape

Frantz started confronting and frightening Ti-Co to the point where he eventually drove him away. He then told Maria that as he was her childhood friend, he taught it unfair that she had made love with other men but never with him. He told her that he had loved her since the first time they met when they were twelve.

Maria thought about what he said and a feeling of guilt set in. She had never given Frantz the time of day simply because he was young and short. She had heard previously from other girls that Frantz was quite good in bed and being she had not had any sex since the delivery six months ago, she made him a proposition.

She told him that; if she gave in and let him make love to her, would he then leave her alone and stop hanging around the cabin. Frantz agreed at once to Maria's invitation and arrangements were made were he would meet her at a friends place to have sex together.

Later that evening, the two met and made love at Maria's friend's cabin. Soon after Maria realized that allowing Frantz to love her was a terrible mistake on her part. Once Frantz had tasted making love to Maria, he was at the cabin every day wanting to have her again and again.

Eventually, Maria became accustomed to having Frantz around and she invited him to be at her side as long as he could provide for the family.

He wanted to be with Maria so he quit school and he in turn became a taxi driver himself to help with the supporting of his new family of five strong.

His parents were furious at him for leaving school and told him that if he went ahead with his plan to leave everything to be with Maria, he would no longer be considered as a part of his own family.

Tears of Blood

He told his parents that that from then on, they were no longer his family and that Maria's family was the only one he had.

For Maria, that created an unhealthy situation where two families now hated and disliked Maria, but under the circumstances that made no difference to her.

She had been trough so many hard times in the past, *that for the time being,* this would still provide a better life for her and the family.

Maria soon discovered that the man she had chosen wasn't by any means the angel he pretended to be. He was insanely jealous of her and he would fight with and chase away any man who dared talk to or even look at her. He acted as if Maria was his wife even though they were never married. Then things got even worse...

One day when Maria was talking to another man on a busy street in Port-au-Prince, Her Frantz pulled up in his taxi and in a fit of jealous anger tore her dress clean off her back and much to her embarrassment, he left her standing in the middle of the street with nothing on but a bra and panties. After he had cooled off, Maria got in his taxi and he took her home.

Some days he would beat her up for no reason but that was the way Haitian men treated their women. After all that was a sign of love wasn't it? Haitian women had to take their men for what they were and that was all there was to it.

If any man dared talk to or even look at Maria, her man would have a fit of jealousy and he would beat up the other guy and chase him away. For a while Maria actually believed that she loved her man regardless of what he did to her. His fits of jealousy must have been a sign of love, *she would think to herself.*

The Final Escape

Another day in a fit of anger, he took the glass cover from the hot oil lamp and pressed it against her arm causing third degree burns to her flesh.

The more she screamed the more he would push the lamp deeper in her flesh. Then seeing the pain he had caused her he would cry and tell her he was sorry for hurting her.

He would promise not hurt her again only to hit her in the face two days later where he would apologies again for hitting her.

Some days she would have swollen eyes caused by the beatings he inflicted on her without reason.

Eventually the relationship turned sour and both of them started seeing and getting involved with other people to a point where that sort of unhealthy couple behavior became a routine part of life.

To top everything off, her man was nothing short of a sex maniac who wanted to make love to her whenever it pleased him and sometimes, this could be three or four times a day or night.

Over a period of a few years, Maria realized that she had to get away from this beast that she had invited into her life. She came to the conclusion that Haiti was no place for her or her daughter Sabrina. Haiti was not a place with a future for any woman of poor descent.

One year later, Diane brought her husband to be to Canada and one year after that, she brought in Joe and Marc the two youngest of the family on student visas.

Both Joe and Marc were then returned to Haiti after their student visas expired but two years later Diane brought in the two youngest brothers on a permanent basis thus keeping her promise to Maria.

Tears of Blood

Maria, Gus, Sergio and daughter Sabrina where the only ones still left in Haiti when Maria decided that there was no life or future for her and her daughter if they stayed in the hell hole ghetto of En-bas-Mapou.

During the past year she had made some powerful friends in the Government and she was able to secure an exit visa for herself. She made the painful decision of leaving for Canada without her precious daughter.

She had little choice but to leave Haiti alone in order to find work abroad. There she could get work and find a suitable home to bring up her daughter where the child would have a future.

Maria had made arrangements for Sabrina to stay with Brutus' wife Gisele until the time where she could bring her daughter to live with her in Canada.

In 1979, Maria got her exit visa and migrated to Ottawa Canada, where she worked as a maid for a well to do couple. In the year that followed Gus and Sergio also migrated to Canada.

One year later, Maria left Ottawa and moved to Montreal where she was close to the family that had all managed to be together again.

In 1982, Maria had a nightmare. She dreamed her dead mother was standing by her bedside staring at her with a look of anger on her face. In the dream, Fania told Maria, *that if she didn't get Sabrina away from Brutus' wife,* then she *(Fania)* would take her away.

The following morning, Maria went and visited Julia in Montreal and told her of the dream she had the previous night. Julia told Maria that she should move her daughter Sabrina away from where she was at once. At that time Sabrina was already eight years old.

The Final Escape

That same day Maria called the man she had left behind in Port-au-Prince and had him go and get Sabrina from Gisele's home. Sabrina stayed several years in the care of Frantz's brother and sister.

During the next year Maria's last two brothers still in Haiti got exit papers and they also migrated to Canada.

During the next few years, Maria discovered that women were treated with dignity and respect when they lived in a society governed by laws. In America, men can't beat women up and get away with it.

She realized that the man, *she though she loved during her last few years in Haiti,* was nothing else but a monster and that she was glad to have gotten rid of him before it would have become too late.

With Julia, Diane and the four brothers all living in Montreal, Maria would constantly meet with them.

Every month, since she had left Haiti, Maria had religiously sent money back to her homeland for the upkeep and care of her daughter Sabrina.

In 1985, Maria had saved up enough money and succeeded in bringing her daughter Sabrina to live with her in Montreal, Canada.

The family never returned to the abject misery they endured in Haiti. However the traumatizing effects suffered by all of them, *during those painful years,* will remain in their minds and haunt them every day, month after month for as long as they all shall live...

- 7 -

The Conclusion

On January 11th 2012, exactly two years less one day following the massive earthquake that devastated Haiti, Maria accompanied by her brother Gus flew to Haiti to visit with the rest of family that she had not seen in some thirty odd years.

This was Maria's first visit to her homeland since leaving Haiti in 1982. Gus acted as a driver guide and bodyguard for Maria during her visit as the conditions in Haiti since the 2010 earthquake made it an unsafe and dangerous destination for any woman travelling alone.

She was astounded to find, that; following the major earthquake in 2010, Haiti was engulfed in a much worse financial and health related crisis compared to when she had lived there in a ghetto some forty/fifty years ago.

During her short one week visit, Maria visited family that lived in tents and make shift cabins with no water or electricity. At one cabins, she met an orphan boy who had lost both of his parents during the devastating 2010 earthquake. They found him wandering the streets and the family took him in as one of their own.

At another cabin where three sick relatives lived, Maria saw one who had a swollen foot the size of a football and he had huge sores on his legs. From a safe distance, Maria noticed that the sores seemed to be moving. When she moved closer to have a better look, she stepped back in horror. There were ants and flies eating away at the poor man's flesh as he looked on...

Tears of Blood

When Maria and Gus left that cabin, Gus turned to her and said... "Sister, we have just left a living cemetery with three live corpses waiting to be buried."

When Maria visited another cabin where twenty-five relatives, men, women and children live, she found smiling people who were so happy to see her. Some of the people in the cabin were only five to ten years old when Maria left Haiti thirty years ago. Some had grown up to be men who had fathered their own children and yet they were still in the same place as where they were thirty years ago. The warm and genuine greeting she got from those poor Souls moved her to tears.

On a road in Pétion-Ville, she saw an old woman sitting on the road begging for food. She sat so close to the passing cars that it was nothing short of a miracle she had not been run-over and killed. When she asked Gus to stop the jeep to help the old lady, Gus replied that there are thousands like her begging for food and that and you simply can't help them all.

As Maria insisted, Gus stopped the jeep and she got out and approached the poor old woman. Maria noticed that the old lady was filthy of dirt and was nothing but a living skeleton of skin and bones.

Please help me; *cried out the old woman,* holding out both hands palm upwards. I am hungry she cried, I haven't eaten in days. Maria was overwhelmed at such a spectacle and when she gave the old woman five dollars, the old beggar tried to kiss Maria's feet. No-don't do that Maria told her. You must never kiss someone's feet for helping you when you are in need.

When Maria turned towards Gus, he noticed that her eyes were full of tears. You have to be tough to visit this hellhole, *he said,* or else it's you that will crumble.

The Conclusion

Maria looked at her brother and said; **"We all suffered Abject Misery in Haiti when we were young, but that was nothing compared to what our remaining families and the poor and destitute people of Haiti are facing today."**

When Maria got back to Montreal, it took several weeks before the memory of the events she had just witnessed in Haiti started fading away. Before her visit to Haiti, Maria was haunted and traumatized by the events following her mother's death and the hell she and her sister and brothers lived through in the Haitian ghettos. Now she would have two events to forget...

Gus had been back to Haiti on many occasions over the years and had become immune to the misery surrounding these people. On January 12th 2010 he had just left the airport for the hotel he had reserved and was standing outside the hotel when the massive earthquake struck Haiti. For a moment he though of his wife and children in Montreal for he believed the world had come to an end and he wondered if his family had died in Montreal. The hotel that he was minutes away from entering had vanished into a pile of dirt, stones and rubble. He had escaped death by a few minutes...

There was so much dirt and dust in the air that he couldn't see more than two feet past his nose.

When he had gotten over the initial shock and realizing he had survived, he whipped the dust from his face and he grabbed both of his legs and squeezed them to see if he was still alive.

Even two years later, Gus still talks about that day when he had believed the world had come to its end.

- - - - - - - - - - - - - - - -

Tears of Blood

For the reader to understand what abject misery can be and what the situation was really like in Haiti at the time of the first printing of this book on January 30th 2012, the reader must go back two years to the events that occurred in Haiti on January 12th 2010.

The **2010 Haiti earthquake** was a catastrophic magnitude 7.0 M_w earthquake, with an epicenter near the town of Léogâne, approximately 25 km (16 miles) west of Port-au-Prince, Haiti's capital. The earthquake occurred at 16:53 local time (21:53 UTC) on Tuesday, 12 January 2010

By 24 January, at least 52 aftershocks measuring 4.5 or greater had been recorded. An estimated three million people were affected by the quake.

The Haitian government reported that an estimated 316,000 people had died, 300,000 had been injured and 1,000,000 made homeless. The government of Haiti also estimated that 250,000 residences and 30,000 commercial buildings had collapsed or were severely damaged.

The earthquake caused major damage in Port-au-Prince, Jacmel and other settlements in the region. Many notable landmark buildings were significantly damaged or destroyed, including the Presidential Palace, the National Assembly building, the Port-au-Prince Cathedral, and the main jail. Among those killed were Archbishop of Port-au-Prince Joseph Serge Miot, and opposition leader Micha Gaillard.

The headquarters of the United Nations Stabilization Mission in Haiti (MINUSTAH), located in the capital, collapsed, killing many, including the Mission's Chief, Hédi Annabi.

The Conclusion

Many countries responded to appeals for humanitarian aid, pledging funds and dispatching rescue and medical teams, engineers and support personnel. Communication systems, air, land, and sea transport facilities, hospitals, and electrical networks had been damaged by the earthquake, which hampered rescue and aid efforts; confusion over who was in charge, air traffic congestion, and problems with prioritisation of flights further complicated early relief work.

Port-au-Prince's morgues were quickly overwhelmed with many tens of thousands of bodies having to be buried in mass graves. As rescues tailed off, supplies, medical care and sanitation became priorities. Delays in aid distribution led to angry appeals from aid workers and survivors, and looting and sporadic violence were observed.

On 22 January the United Nations noted that the emergency phase of the relief operation was drawing to a close, and on the following day the Haitian government officially called off the search for survivors.

"Background"

The island of Hispaniola, shared by Haiti and the Dominican Republic, is seismically active and has a history of destructive earthquakes.

During Haiti's time as a French colony, earthquakes were recorded by French historian Moreau de Saint-Méry (1750–1819). He described damage done by an earthquake in 1751, writing that "only one masonry building had not collapsed" in Port-au-Prince; he also wrote that the "whole city collapsed" in the 1770 Port-au-Prince earthquake.

Tears of Blood

Cap-Haïtien, other towns in the north of Haiti and the Dominican Republic, and the Sans-Souci Palace were destroyed during an earthquake on 7 May 1842.

A magnitude 8.0 earthquake struck the Dominican Republic and shook Haiti on 4 August 1946, producing a tsunami that killed 1,790 people and injured many others.

Haiti is ranked 149th of 182 countries on the Human Development Index and is the poorest country in the Western Hemisphere. The Australian government's travel advisory site had previously expressed concerns that Haitian emergency services would be unable to cope in the event of a major disaster, and the country is considered "economically vulnerable" by the Food and Agriculture Organization. It is no stranger to natural disasters; in addition to earthquakes, it has been struck frequently by tropical cyclones, which have caused extreme flooding and widespread collateral damage.

The most recent cyclones to hit the island before the earthquake were Tropical Storm Fay and Hurricanes Gustav, Hanna and Ike, all in the summer of 2008, causing nearly 800 deaths.

A magnitude 7.0 M_w earthquake occurred inland, on 12 January 2010 at 16:53 (UTC-05:00), approximately 25 kilometres (16 mi) WSW from Port-au-Prince at a depth of 13 kilometres (8.1 mi) on blind thrust faults associated with the Enriquillo-Plantain Garden fault system. There is no evidence of surface rupture and based on seismological, geological and ground deformation data it is thought that the earthquake did not involve significant lateral slip on the main Enriquillo fault. Strong shaking associated with intensity IX on the Modified Mercalli scale (MM) was recorded in Port-au-Prince and its suburbs.

The Conclusion

The quake was also felt in several surrounding countries and regions, including Cuba (MM III in Guantánamo), Jamaica (MM II in Kingston), Venezuela (MM II in Caracas), Puerto Rico (MM II–III in San Juan), and the bordering Dominican Republic (MM III in Santo Domingo). According to estimates from the United States Geological Survey, approximately 3.5 million people lived in the area that experienced shaking intensity of MM VII to X, a range that can cause moderate to very heavy damage even to earthquake-resistant structures.

The damage from the quake was more severe than for other quakes of similar magnitude due to the shallow depth of the quake.

The quake occurred in the vicinity of the northern boundary where the Caribbean tectonic plate shifts eastwards by about 20 millimetres (0.79 in) per year in relation to the North American plate.

The strike-slip fault system in the region has two branches in Haiti, the Septentrional-Oriente fault in the north and the Enriquillo-Plantain Garden fault in the south; both its location and focal mechanism suggested that the January 2010 quake was caused by a rupture of the Enriquillo-Plantain Garden fault, which had been locked for 250 years, gathering stress. However, a study published in May 2010 suggested that the rupture process may have involved slip on multiple blind thrust faults with only minor, deep, lateral slip along or near the main Enriquillo–Plantain Garden fault zone, suggesting that the event only partially relieved centuries of accumulated left-lateral strain on a small part of the plate-boundary system. The rupture was roughly 65 kilometres (40 mi) long with mean slip of 1.8 metres (5.9 ft).

Preliminary analysis of the slip distribution found amplitudes of up to about 4 metres (13 ft) using ground motion records from all over the world.

A 2007 earthquake hazard study by C. DeMets and M. Wiggins-Grandison noted that the Enriquillo-Plantain Garden fault zone could be at the end of its seismic cycle and concluded that a worst-case forecast would involve a 7.2 M_w earthquake, similar in size to the 1692 Jamaica earthquake. Paul Mann and a group including the 2006 study team presented a hazard assessment of the Enriquillo-Plantain Garden fault system to the 18th Caribbean Geologic Conference in March 2008, noting the large strain; the team recommended "high priority" historical geologic rupture studies, as the fault was fully locked and had recorded few earthquakes in the preceding 40 years. An article published in Haiti's *Le Matin* newspaper in September 2008 cited comments by geologist Patrick Charles to the effect that there was a high risk of major seismic activity in Port-au-Prince.

The United States Geological Survey (USGS) recorded eight aftershocks in the two hours after the main earthquake, with magnitudes between 4.3 and 5.9. Within the first nine hours 32 aftershocks of magnitude 4.2 or greater were recorded, 12 of which measured magnitude 5.0 or greater, and on January 24 USGS reported that there had been 52 aftershocks measuring 4.5 or greater since the January 12 quake.

On 20 January at 06:03 local time (11:03 UTC) the strongest aftershock since the earthquake, measuring magnitude 5.9 M_w, struck Haiti. USGS reported its epicenter was about 56 kilometres (35 mi) WSW of Port-au-Prince, which would place it almost exactly under the coastal town of Petit-Goâve.

The Conclusion

A UN representative reported that the aftershock collapsed seven buildings in the town.

According to staff of the International Committee of the Red Cross, which had reached Petit-Goâve for the first time the day before the aftershock, the town was estimated to have lost 15% of its buildings, and was suffering the same shortages of supplies and medical care as the capital. Workers from the charity Save the Children reported hearing "already weakened structures collapsing" in Port-au-Prince, but most sources reported no further significant damage to infrastructure in the city.

Further casualties are thought to have been minimal since people had been sleeping in the open. There are concerns that the 12 January earthquake could be the beginning of a new long-term sequence: "the whole region is fearful"; historical accounts, although not precise, suggest that there has been a sequence of quakes progressing westwards along the fault, starting with an earthquake in the Dominican Republic in 1751.

"Tsunami"

The Pacific Tsunami Warning Center issued a tsunami warning immediately after the initial quake, but quickly cancelled it. Nearly two weeks later it was reported that the beach of the small fishing town of Petit Paradis was hit by a localised tsunami wave shortly after the earthquake, probably as a result of an underwater slide, and this was later confirmed by researchers. At least three people were swept out to sea by the wave and were reported dead. Witnesses told reporters that the sea first retreated and a "very big wave" followed rapidly, crashing ashore and sweeping boats and debris into the ocean.

Tears of Blood

Amongst the widespread devastation and damage throughout Port-au-Prince and elsewhere, vital infrastructure necessary to respond to the disaster was severely damaged or destroyed.

This included all hospitals in the capital; air, sea, and land transport facilities; and communication systems.

The quake affected the three Médecins Sans Frontières (Doctors Without Borders) medical facilities around Port-au-Prince, causing one to collapse completely. A hospital in Pétionville, a wealthy suburb of Port-au-Prince, also collapsed, as did the St. Michel District Hospital in the southern town of Jacmel, which was the largest referral hospital in south-east Haiti.

The quake seriously damaged the control tower at Toussaint L'Ouverture International Airport and the Port-au-Prince seaport, which rendered the harbor unusable for immediate rescue operations. The Gonaïves seaport, in the northern part of Haiti, remained operational.

Roads were blocked with road debris or the surfaces broken. The main road linking Port-au-Prince with Jacmel remained blocked ten days after the earthquake, hampering delivery of aid to Jacmel. When asked why the road had not been opened, Hazem el-Zein, head of the south-east division of the UN World Food Programme said that "We ask the same questions to the people in charge...They promise rapid response. To be honest, I don't know why it hasn't been done. I can only think that their priority must be somewhere else."

There was considerable damage to communications infrastructure. The public telephone system was not available.

The Conclusion

Two of Haiti's largest cellular telephone providers, Digicel and Comcel Haiti, both reported that their services had been affected by the earthquake.

Fibre-optic connectivity had also been disrupted. According to Reporters Sans Frontières (RSF), Radio Lumière, which broadcasts out of Port-au-Prince and reaches 90% of Haiti, was initially knocked off the air, but it was able to resume broadcasting across most of its network within a week.

According to RSF, some 20 of about 50 stations that were active in the capital region prior to the earthquake were back on air a week after the quake.

Large portions of the National Palace collapsed and in February 2010 Prime Minister Jean-Max Bellerive estimated that 250,000 residences and 30,000 commercial buildings were severely damaged and needed to be demolished.

The deputy mayor of Léogâne reported that 90% of the town's buildings had been destroyed. Many government and public buildings were damaged or including the Palace of Justice, the National Assembly, the Supreme Court and Port-au-Prince Cathedral.

The National Palace was severely damaged, though President René Préval and his wife Elisabeth Delatour Préval escaped injury. The Prison Civile de Port-au-Prince was also destroyed, allowing around 4,000 inmates to escape.

Most of Port-au-Prince's municipal buildings were destroyed or heavily damaged, including the City Hall, which was described by the *Washington Post* as, "a skeletal hulk of concrete and stucco, sagging grotesquely to the left."

Tears of Blood

Port-au-Prince had no municipal petrol reserves and few city officials had working mobile phones before the earthquake, complicating both communications and transportation. Minister of Education Joel Jean-Pierre stated that the education system had "totally collapsed". About half the nation's schools and the three main universities in Port-au-Prince were affected. More than 1,300 schools and 50 health care facilities were destroyed.

The earthquake also destroyed a nursing school in the capital and severely damaged the country's primary midwifery school. The Haitian art world suffered great losses; artworks were destroyed, and museums and art galleries were extensively damaged, among them Port-au-Prince's main art museum, Centre d'Art, College Saint Pierre and Holy Trinity Cathedral.

The headquarters of the United Nations Stabilization Mission in Haiti (MINUSTAH) at Christopher Hotel and offices of the World Bank were destroyed. The building housing the offices of Citibank in Port-au-Prince collapsed, killing five employees. The clothing industry, which accounts for two-thirds of Haiti's exports, reported structural damage at most of its manufacturing facilities.

The quake created a landslide dam on the Rivière de Grand Goâve. As of February 2010 the water level was low, but engineer Yves Gattereau believed the dam could collapse during the rainy season, which would flood Grand-Goâve 12 kilometres (7.5 mi) downstream.

In the nights following the earthquake, many people in Haiti slept in the streets, on pavements, in their cars, or in makeshift shanty towns either because their houses had been destroyed, or they feared standing structures would not withstand aftershocks.

The Conclusion

Construction standards are low in Haiti; the country has no building codes. Engineers have stated that it is unlikely many buildings would have stood through any kind of disaster. Structures are often raised wherever they can fit; some buildings were built on slopes with insufficient foundations or steel works.

A representative of the Catholic Relief Services has estimated that about two million Haitians lived as squatters on land they did not own. The country also suffered from shortages of fuel and potable water even before the disaster.

President Préval and government ministers used police headquarters near the Toussaint L'Ouverture International Airport as their new base of operations, although their effectiveness was extremely limited; several parliamentarians were still trapped in the Presidential Palace, and offices and records had been destroyed. Some high-ranking government workers lost family members, or had to tend to wounded relatives.

Although the president and his remaining cabinet met with UN planners each day, there remained confusion as to who was in charge and no single group had organized relief efforts as of 16 January.

The government handed over control of the airport to the United States to hasten and ease flight operations, which had been hampered by the damage to the air traffic control tower.

Almost immediately all of Port-au-Prince's morgue facilities were overwhelmed. By 14 January, a thousand bodies had been placed on the streets and pavements. Government crews manned trucks to collect thousands more, burying them in mass graves.

Tears of Blood

In the heat and humidity, corpses buried in rubble began to decompose and smell. Mati Goldstein, head of the Israeli ZAKA International Rescue Unit delegation to Haiti, described the situation as "Shabbat from hell.

Everywhere, the acrid smell of bodies hangs in the air. It's just like the stories we are told of the Holocaust – thousands of bodies everywhere. You have to understand that the situation is true madness, and the more time passes, there are more and more bodies, in numbers that cannot be grasped. It is beyond comprehension."

Mayor Jean-Yves Jason said that officials argued for hours about what to do with the volume of corpses. The government buried many in mass graves, some above-ground tombs were forced open so bodies could be stacked inside, and others were burned. Mass graves were dug in a large field outside the settlement of Titanyen, north of the capital; tens of thousands of bodies were reported as having been brought to the site by dump truck and buried in trenches dug by earth movers. Max Beauvoir, a voodoo priest, protested the lack of dignity in mass burials, stating, "... it is not in our culture to bury people in such a fashion, it is desecration". But in such a situation there is little choice

The Haitian government began a program to move homeless people out of Port-au-Prince on a ferry to Port Jeremie and in hired buses to temporary camps.

Towns in the eastern Dominican Republic began preparing for tens of thousands of refugees, and by 16 January hospitals close to the border had been filled to capacity with Haitians.

Some began reporting having expended stocks of critical medical supplies such as antibiotics by Jan 17.

The Conclusion

The border was reinforced by Dominican soldiers, and the government of the Dominican Republic asserted that all Haitians who crossed the border for medical assistance would be allowed to stay only temporarily.

A local governor stated, "We have a great desire and we will do everything humanly possible to help Haitian families. But we have our limitations with respect to food and medicine. We need the helping hand of other countries in the area."

Slow distribution of resources in the days after the earthquake resulted in sporadic violence, with looting reported. There were also accounts of looters wounded or killed by vigilantes and neighborhoods that had constructed their own roadblock barricades.

Dr Evan Lyon of Partners in Health, working at the General Hospital in Port-au-Prince, claimed that misinformation and overblown reports of violence had hampered the delivery of aid and medical services.

Former U.S. president Bill Clinton was overwhelmed by the massive destruction he had witnessed and acknowledged the problems and said Americans should "not be deterred from supporting the relief effort" by upsetting scenes such as those of looting.

Lt. Gen. P.K. Keen, deputy commander of U.S. Southern Command, however, announced that despite the stories of looting and violence, there was less violent crime in Port-au-Prince after the earthquake than before.

In many neighborhoods, singing could be heard through the night and groups of men coordinated to act as security as groups of women attempted to take care of food and hygiene necessities.

Tears of Blood

During the days following the earthquake, hundreds were seen marching through the streets in peaceful processions, singing and clapping.

The earthquake caused an urgent need for outside rescuers to communicate with Haitians whose main or only language is Haitian Creole. As a result, a machine translation program to translate between English and Haitian Creole had to be written quickly.

The earthquake struck in the most populated area of the country. The International Federation of Red Cross and Red Crescent Societies estimated that as many as 3 million people had been affected by the quake. In mid February 2010, the Haitian government reported the death toll to have reached 230,000. However, an investigation by Radio Netherlands has questioned the official death toll, reporting an estimate of 92,000 deaths as being a more realistic figure. On the first anniversary of the earthquake, 12 January 2011, Haitian Prime Minister Jean-Max Bellerive said the death toll from the quake was more than 316,000, raising the figures from previous estimates.

Several experts have questioned the validity of the death toll numbers; Anthony Penna, professor emeritus in environmental history at Northeastern University, warned that casualty estimates could only be a guest...

Belgian disaster response expert Claude de Ville de Goyet noted that "round numbers are a sure sign that nobody knows." Edmond Mulet, UN Assistant Secretary-General for Peacekeeping Operations, said, "I do not think we will ever know what the death toll is from this earthquake", while the director of the Haitian Red Cross, Guiteau Jean-Pierre, noted that his organization had not had the time to count bodies, as their focus had been on the treatment of survivors.

The Conclusion

While the vast majority of casualties were Haitian civilians, the dead included aid workers, embassy staff, foreign tourists—and a number of public figures, including the Archbishop of Port-au-Prince Monsignor Joseph Serge Miot, aid worker Zilda Arns and officials in the Haitian government, including opposition leader Michel "Micha" Gaillard.

Also killed were a number of well-known Haitian musicians and sports figures, including thirty members of the Fédération Haïtienne de Football. At least 85 United Nations personnel working with MINUSTAH were killed, among them the Mission Chief, Hédi Annabi, his deputy, Luiz Carlos da Costa., and police commissioner Douglas Coates. Around 200 guests were killed in the collapse of the Hôtel Montana in Port-au-Prince.

On 31 May 2011, an unreleased draft report based on a survey commissioned by the US Agency for International Development (USAID) challenged the Haiti earthquake death toll and several damage estimates. The unpublished report put the death toll between 46,000 and 85,000 and put the number of displaced persons at 895,000, of which only 375,000 remained in temporary shelters. The unreleased report, which compiled its figures from a door-to-door survey, was done by a Washington consulting firm, LTL Strategies.

A US State Department spokesperson said the report had inconsistencies and would not be released until they were resolved. As of January 2012, USAID has not released the report and states at its website that 1.5 million people were displaced, of which 550,000 remain without permanent shelter.

Appeals for humanitarian aid were issued by many aid organizations, the United Nations and president René Préval.

Tears of Blood

Raymond Joseph, Haiti's ambassador to the United States, and his nephew, singer Wyclef Jean, who was called upon by Préval to become a "roving ambassador" for Haiti, also pleaded for aid and donations.

Many countries responded to the appeals and launched fund-raising efforts, as well as sending search and rescue teams. The neighboring Dominican Republic was the first country to give aid to Haiti, sending water, food and heavy-lifting machinery.

The hospitals in the Dominican Republic were made available; a combined effort of the Airports Department (DA), together with the Dominican Naval Auxiliaries, the UN and other parties formed the Dominican-Haitian Aerial Support Bridge, making the main Dominican airports available for support operations to Haiti.

The Dominican website FlyDominicanRepublic.com made available to the internet, daily updates on airport information and news from the operations center on the Dominican side. The Dominican emergency team assisted more than 2,000 injured people, while the Dominican Institute of Telecommunications (Indotel) helped with the restoration of some telephone services.

The Dominican Red Cross coordinated early medical relief in conjunction with the International Red Cross.

The government sent eight mobile medical units along with 36 doctors including orthopaedics specialists, traumatologists, anaesthetist, and surgeons.

In addition, 39 trucks carrying canned food were dispatched, along with 10 mobile kitchens and 110 cooks capable of producing 100,000 meals per day.

Other nations from farther afield also sent personnel, medicines, materiel, and other aid to Haiti.

The conclusion

The first team to arrive in Port-au-Prince was ICE-SAR from Iceland, landing within 24 hours of the earthquake. A 50-member Chinese team arrived early Thursday morning. From the Middle East, the government of Qatar sent a strategic transport aircraft (C-17), loaded with 50 tons of urgent relief materials and 26 members from the Qatari armed forces, the internal security force (Lekhwiya), police force and the Hamad Medical Corporation, to set up a field hospital and provide assistance in Port-au-Prince and other affected areas in Haiti.

A rescue team sent by the Israel Defense Forces' Home Front Command established a field hospital near the United Nations building in Port-au-Prince with specialised facilities to treat children, the elderly, and women in labor. It was set up in eight hours and began operations on the evening of 16 January.

A Korean International Disaster Relief Team with 40 rescuers, medical doctors, nurses and 2 k-9s was deployed to epicenters to assist mitigation efforts of Haitian Government.

The American Red Cross announced on 13 January that it had run out of supplies in Haiti and appealed for public donations. Giving Children Hope worked to get much-needed medicines and supplies on the ground.

Partners in Health, (PIH), the largest health care provider in rural Haiti, was able to provide some emergency care from its ten hospitals and clinics, all of which were outside the capital and undamaged. MINUSTAH had over 9,000 uniformed peacekeepers deployed to the area. Most of these workers were initially involved in the search for survivors at the organization's collapsed headquarters.

Tears of Blood

The International Charter on Space and Major Disasters was activated, allowing satellite imagery of affected regions to be shared with rescue and aid organizations. Members of social networking sites such as Twitter and Facebook spread messages and pleas to send help. Facebook was overwhelmed by—and blocked—some users who were sending messages about updates. The American Red Cross set a record for mobile donations, raising US$7 million in 24 hours when they allowed people to send US$10 donations by text messages.

The Open Street Map community responded to the disaster by greatly improving the level of mapping available for the area using post-earthquake satellite photography provided by GeoEye, and tracking website Ushahidi coordinated messages from multiple sites to assist Haitians still trapped and to keep families of survivors informed. Some online poker sites, hosted poker tournaments with tournament fees, prizes or both going to disaster relief charities. Google Earth updated its coverage of Port-au-Prince on 17 January, showing the earthquake-ravaged city.

Easing refugee immigration into Canada was discussed by Canadian Prime Minister Stephen Harper, and in the U.S., 100,000 illegal alien Haitians were granted Temporary Protected Status.

This was a measure that permits about 100,000 illegal alien Haitians in the United States to stay legally for 18 months, and halts the deportations of 30,000 more, though it does not apply to Haitians outside the U.S. Local and state agencies in South Florida, together with the U.S. government, began implementing a plan ("Operation Vigilant Sentry") for a mass migration from the Caribbean that had been laid out in 2003.

The Conclusion

Several orphanages were completely destroyed in the earthquake. After the process for the adoption of 400 children by families in the U.S. and the Netherlands was expedited, Unicef and SOS Children urged an immediate halt to adoptions from Haiti. Jasmine Whitbread, chief executive of Save the Children said: "The vast majority of the children currently on their own still have family members alive who will be desperate to be reunited with them and will be able to care for them with the right support. Taking children out of the country would permanently separate thousands of children from their families—a separation that would compound the acute trauma they are already suffering and inflict long-term damage on their chances of recovery." However, several organizations were planning an airlift of thousands of orphaned children to South Florida on humanitarian visas, modelled on a similar effort with Cuban refugees in the 1960s named "Pedro Pan". The Canadian government worked to expedite around 100 adoption cases that were already underway when the earthquake struck, issuing temporary permits and waving regular processing fees; the federal government also announced that it would cover adopted children's healthcare costs upon their arrival in Canada until they could be covered under provincially-administered public healthcare plans.

Rescue efforts began in the immediate aftermath of the earthquake, with able-bodied survivors extricating the living and the dead from the rubble of the many buildings that had collapsed. Treatment of the injured was hampered by the lack of hospital and morgue facilities: the Argentine military field hospital, which had been serving MINUSTAH, was the only one available until 13 January.

Tears of Blood

Rescue work intensified only slightly with the arrival of doctors, police officers, military personnel and firefighters from various countries two days after the earthquake.

From 12 January, the International Committee of the Red Cross, which has been working in Haiti since 1994, focused on bringing emergency assistance to victims of the catastrophe, in close cooperation with its partners within the International Red Cross and Red Crescent Movement, particularly the Haitian Red Cross and the International Federation of Red Cross and Red Crescent Societies.

Médecins Sans Frontières (Doctors Without Borders; MSF) reported that the hospitals that had not been destroyed were overwhelmed by large numbers of seriously injured people, and that they had to carry out many amputations. Running short of medical supplies, some teams had to work with any available resources, constructing splints out of cardboard and reusing latex gloves. Other rescue units had to withdraw as night fell amid security fears. Over 3,000 people had been treated by Médecins Sans Frontières as of 18 January.

Ophelia Dahl, director of Partners in Health, reported, "there are hundreds of thousands of injured people. I have heard the estimate that as many as 20,000 people will die each day that would have been saved by surgery."

An MSF aircraft carrying a field hospital was repeatedly turned away by U.S. air traffic controllers who had assumed control at Toussaint L'Ouverture International Airport. Four other MSF aircraft were also turned away. In a 19 January press release, MSF said, "It is like working in a war situation. We don't have any more morphine to manage pain for our patients.

The Conclusion

We cannot accept that planes carrying lifesaving medical supplies and equipment continue to be turned away while our patients die. Priority must be given to medical supplies entering the country." First responders voiced frustration with the number of relief trucks sitting unused at the airport. Aid workers blamed U.S.-controlled airport operations for prioritising the transportation of security troops over rescuers and supplies; evacuation policies favoring citizens of certain nations were also criticised.

The U.S. military acknowledged the non-governmental organizations' complaints concerning flight-operations bias and promised improvement while noting that up to 17 January 600 emergency flights had landed and 50 were diverted; by the first weekend of disaster operations diversions had been reduced to three on Saturday and two on Sunday.

The airport was able to support 100 landings a day, up from the 35 a day that the airport gets during normal operation. A spokesman for the joint task force running the airport confirmed that though more flights were requesting landing slots, none were being turned away.

Brazilian Foreign Minister Celso Amorim and French Minister of State for Cooperation Alain Joyandet criticised the perceived preferential treatment for U.S. aid arriving at the airport.

A spokesman for the French Ministry of Foreign Affairs said that there had been no official protest from the French government with regard to the management of the airport. U.S. officials acknowledged that coordination of the relief effort is central to Haitian recovery, and Haiti's President Préval asked for calm coordination between assisting nations

Tears of Blood

President Préval also asked that errors or accidents should be without judgment or mutual accusations.

While international efforts received significant media coverage, much of the rescue effort was conducted by Haitians themselves

While the Port-au-Prince airport ramp has spaces for over a dozen airliners, in the days following the quake it sometimes served nearly 40 at once, creating serious delays.

The supply backup at the airport was expected to ease as the apron management improved, and when the perceived need for heavy security diminished. Airport congestion was reduced further on 18 January when the United Nations and U.S. forces formally agreed to prioritise humanitarian flights over security reinforcement.

By 14 January, over 20 countries had sent military personnel to the country, with Canada, the United States and the Dominican Republic providing the largest contingents. The supercarrier USS *Carl Vinson* arrived at maximum possible speed on 15 January with 600,000 emergency food rations, 100,000 ten-litre water containers, and with an enhanced wing of 19 helicopters; 130,000 litres of drinking water were transferred to shore on the first day.

The helicopter carrier USS *Bataan* sailed with three large dock landing ships and two survey/salvage vessels, to create a "sea base" for the rescue effort.

They were joined by the French Navy vessel *Francis Garnier* on 16 January, the same day the hospital ship USNS *Comfort* and guided-missile cruiser USS *Bunker Hill* left for Haiti. Another large French vessel was later ordered to Haiti, the amphibious transport dock *Siroco*.

The Conclusion

International rescue efforts were restricted by traffic congestion and blocked roads. Although U.S. Secretary of Defense Robert Gates had previously ruled out dropping food and water by air as too dangerous, by 16 January, U.S. helicopters were distributing aid to areas impossible to reach by land.

In Jacmel, a city of 50,000, the mayor claimed that 70% of the homes had been damaged and that the quake had killed 300 to 500 people and left some 4,000 injured. The small airstrip had suffered damage that rendered it totally unusable for supply flights until 20 January. The Canadian navy vessel HMCS *Halifax* was deployed to the area on 18 January; the Canadians joined Colombian rescue workers, Chilean doctors, a French mobile clinic, and Sri Lankan relief workers who had already responded to calls for aid.

About 64,000 people living in the three adjacent agricultural communities of Durissy, Morne a Chandelle, and Les Palmes were relatively unharmed because most of the people were working in the fields; but all churches, chapels and at least 8,000 homes were destroyed.

British search and rescue teams were the first to arrive in Léogane, the town at the epicenter of the quake, on 17 January. The Canadian ship HMCS *Athabaskan* reached the area on 19 January, and by 20 January there were 250-300 Canadian personnel assisting relief efforts in the town.

By 19 January, staff of the International Red Cross had also managed to reach the town, which they described as "severely damaged ... the people there urgently need assistance", and by 20 January they had reached Petit-Goâve as well, where they set up two first-aid posts and distributed first-aid kits.

Tears of Blood

Over the first weekend 130,000 food packets and 70,000 water containers were distributed to Haitians, as safe landing areas and distribution centers such as golf courses were secured. There were nearly 2,000 rescuers present from 43 different groups, with 161 search dogs; the airport had handled 250 tons of relief supplies by the end of the weekend. Reports from Sunday showed a record-breaking number of successful rescues, with at least 12 survivors pulled from Port-au-Prince's rubble, bringing the total number of rescues to 110.

The buoy tender USCG *Oak* and USNS *Grasp* (T-ARS-51) were on scene by 18 January to assess damage to the port and work to reopen it, and by 21 January one pier at the Port-au-Prince seaport was functional, offloading humanitarian aid, and a road had been repaired to make transport into the city easier.

In an interview on 21 January, Leo Merores, Haiti's ambassador to the UN, said that he expected the port to be fully functional again within two weeks.

The U.S. Navy listed its resources in the area as "17 ships, 48 helicopters and 12 fixed-wing aircraft" in addition to 10,000 sailors and Marines. The Navy had conducted 336 air deliveries, delivered 32,400 US gallons (123,000 l; 27,000 imp gal) of water, 532,440 bottles of water, 111,082 meals and 9,000 lb (4,100 kg) of medical supplies by 20 January.

Hospital ship *Comfort* began its operations on 20 January, completing the arrival of the first group of sea-base vessels; this came as a new flotilla of USN ships were assigned to Haiti, including survey vessels, ferries, elements of the maritime prepositioning and underway replenishment fleets.

The Conclusion

Also three further amphibious operations ships, including another helicopter carrier, USS *Nassau* (LHA-4) were included in the operation.

On 22 January the UN and United States formalised the coordination of relief efforts by signing an agreement giving the U.S. responsibility for the ports, airports and roads, and making the UN and Haitian authorities responsible for law and order. The UN stated that it had resisted formalising the organization of the relief effort to allow as much leeway as possible for those wishing to assist in the relief effort, but with the new agreement "we're leaving that emergency phase behind". The UN also urged organizations to coordinate aid efforts through its mission in Haiti to allow for better scheduling of the arrival of supplies.

On 23 January the Haitian government officially called off the search for survivors, and most search and rescue teams began to prepare to leave the country. However, as late as 8 February 2010, survivors were still being discovered, as in the case of Evan Muncie, 28, found in the rubble of a grocery store.

On 5 February, ten Baptist missionaries from Idaho led by Laura Silsby were charged with criminal association and kidnapping for trying to smuggle 33 children out of Haiti. The missionaries claimed they were rescuing orphaned children but investigations revealed that more than 20 of the children had been taken from their parents after they were told the children would have a better life in America.

In an interview, the United States Ambassador to Haiti Kenneth Merten, stated that the U.S. justice system would not interfere and that "the Haitian justice system will do what it has to do."

Tears of Blood

By 9 March 2010, all missionaries but Silsby were deported from Haiti while she remained incarcerated.

Social networking organizations such as Crisis Camp Haiti were developed to aid in the structure and coordination of relief efforts in Haiti and future catastrophic events as well.

On 10 April, due to the potential threat of mudslides and flooding from the upcoming rainy season, the Haitian government began operations to move thousands of refugees to a more secure location north of the capital.

"The recovery"

U.S. President Barack Obama announced that former presidents Bill Clinton, who also acts as the UN special envoy to Haiti, and George W. Bush would coordinate efforts to raise funds for Haiti's recovery. Secretary of State Hillary Clinton visited Haiti on 16 January to survey the damage and stated that US$48 million had been raised already in the U.S. to help Haiti recover. Following the meeting with Secretary Clinton, President Préval stated that the highest priorities in Haiti's recovery were establishing a working government, clearing roads, and ensuring the streets were cleared of bodies to improve sanitary conditions.

U.S. Vice President Joe Biden stated on 16 January that President Obama "does not view this as a humanitarian mission with a life cycle of a month. This will still be on our radar screen long after it's off the crawler at CNN. This is going to be a long slog."

Trade and Industry Minister Josseline Colimon Fethiere estimated that the earthquake's toll on the Haitian economy would be massive, with one out of every five jobs being lost.

The Conclusion

In response to the earthquake, foreign governments offered badly needed financial aid. The European Union promised €330 million for emergency and long-term aid. Brazil announced R$375 million for long-term recovery aid, R$25 million of which in immediate funds.

The United Kingdom's Secretary of State for International Development Douglas Alexander called the result of the earthquake an "almost unprecedented level of devastation", and committed the UK to £20 million in aid, while France promised €10 million.

Italy announced it would waive repayment of the €40 million it had loaned to Haiti, and the World Bank waived the country's debt repayments for five years. On 14 January, the U.S. government announced it would give US$100 million to the aid effort and pledged that the people of Haiti "will not be forgotten".

In the aftermath of the earthquake, the government of Canada announced that it would match the donations of Canadians up to a total of C$50 million. After a United Nations call for help for the people affected by the earthquake, Canada pledged an additional C$60 million in aid on 19 January 2010, bringing Canada's total contribution to C$135 million.

By 8 February 2010, the federal International Co-operation Department, through the Canadian International Development Agency (CIDA), had already provided about C$85 million in humanitarian aid through UN agencies, the International Federation of Red Cross and Red Crescent Societies and to organizations such as CARE, Médecins du Monde, Save the Children, Oxfam Quebec, the Centre for International Studies and Co-operation, and World Vision.

Tears of Blood

On 23 January 2010, Canadian Prime Minister Stephen Harper announced that the federal government had lifted the limit on the amount of money allocated for matching individual donations to relief efforts, and that the federal government would continue to match individual donations until 12 February 2010; by the deadline, Canadians had privately raised C$220 million.

On top of matching donations, International Co-operation Minister Bev Oda pledged an additional C$290 million in long-term relief to be spent between 2010 and 2012, including C$8 million in debt relief to Haiti, part of a broader cancellation of the country's overall World Bank debt.

The Canadian government's commitment to provide C$550 million in aid and debt relief also included Canadians' individual donations amount to a total of CAD$770 million.

In addition to Canada's federal government, the governments of several of the provinces and territories of Canada also announced that they would provide immediate emergency aid to Haiti. On 18 January 2010, the province of Quebec, whose largest city - Montreal - houses the world's largest Haitian diaspora, pledged C$3 million in emergency aid. Both the provincial government of Quebec and the Canadian federal government reaffirmed their commitment to rebuilding Haiti at the 2010 Francophonie Summit; Prime Minister Harper used his opening speech to "tell the head of the Haitian delegation to keep up their spirits" and to urge other nations to continue to support recovery efforts.

President Abdoulaye Wade of Senegal offered interested Haitians free land in Senegal; depending on how many respond to the offer, this could include up to an entire region

The Conclusion

Prime Minister Bellerive announced that from 20 January, people would be helped to relocate outside the zone of devastation, to areas where they may be able to rely on relatives or better fend for themselves.

People who have been made homeless would be relocated to the makeshift camps created by residents within the city, where a more focused delivery of aid and sanitation could be achieved. Port-au-Prince, according to an international studies professor at the University of Miami, was ill-equipped before the disaster to sustain the number of people who had migrated there from the countryside over the past ten years to find work. After the earthquake, thousands of Port-au-Prince residents began returning to the rural towns they came from.

On 25 January a one-day conference was held in Montreal to assess the relief effort and discuss further plans. Prime Minister Bellerive told delegates from 20 countries that Haiti would need "massive support" for its recovery from the international community.

A donors' conference was expected to be held at the UN headquarters in New York in March, however, it took more than three months to hold the UN conference. The 26-member international Interim Haiti Reconstruction Commission, headed by Bill Clinton and Haitian Prime Minister Jean-Max Bellerive, convened in June 2010. That committee is overseeing the $5.3 billion pledged internationally for the first two years of Haiti's reconstruction.

The Netherlands sponsored a project, called Radio555. The Dutch radio channels 3FM, Radio 538 and Radio Veronica all broadcast under the name of Radio555, funded by a contribution of €80 million.

Tears of Blood

Several organizations of the U.S. building industry and government, such as the U.S. Department of Homeland Security and the International Code Council, among others, reported that they were compiling a "Haiti Toolkit" coordinated by the National Institute of Building Sciences.

The toolkit would comprise building technology resources and best practices for consideration by the Haitian government with the goal of creating a more resilient infrastructure to prevent future losses of life.

Immediately following the 2010 earthquake, Real Medicine Foundation began providing medical staffing, in-kind medical supplies and strategic coordination to help meet the surging needs of the health crisis on the ground.

Working in a close partnership with other relief organizations, Real Medicine organized deployments of volunteer medical specialists to meet the needs of partner hospitals and clinics at the Haiti–Dominican Republic border and in Port-au-Prince.

This provided direct funding, medical supplies and pharmaceuticals to local health facilities and partner hospitals, provided advisory services and coordination to local health facilities, including physical therapy support, and coordinated mobile health outreaches, field clinics and food supplies to outlying villages overlooked in the relief effort.

On 15 January 2011, the Catholic Relief Services announced a US$200 million (€195 million), five-year relief and reconstruction program that covers shelter, health, livelihoods, and child protection among its program areas...

The Conclusion

"Status of the recovery"

Six months after the quake as much as 98% of the rubble remained un-cleared. An estimated 26 million cubic yards (20 million cubic meters) remained, making most of the capital impassable, and thousands of bodies remained in the rubble. The number of people in relief camps of tents and tarps since the quake was 1.6 million, and almost no transitional housing had been built.

Most of the camps had no electricity, running water, or sewage disposal, and the tents were beginning to fall apart. Crime in the camps was widespread, especially against women and girls. Between 23 major charities, $1.1 billion had been collected for Haiti for relief efforts, but only two percent of the money had been released.

According to a CBS report, $3.1 billion had been pledged for humanitarian aid and was used to pay for field hospitals, plastic tarps, bandages, and food, plus salaries, transportation and upkeep of relief workers. By May 2010, enough aid had been raised internationally to give each displaced family a check for $37,000.

In July 2010, CNN returned to Port-au-Prince and reported, "It looks like the quake just happened yesterday", and Imogen Wall, spokeswoman for the United Nations office of humanitarian affairs in Haiti, said that six months from that time it may still look the same. The Haitian government said it was unable to tackle debris clean-up or the resettlement of the homeless because they needed to prepare for the hurricane season. Haitian Prime Minister Jean-Max Bellerive stated, "The real priority of the government is to protect the population from the next hurricane season, and most of our effort right now is going right now in that direction."

Tears of Blood

Speaking of the difficulties of living in one of the many camps, one refugee told a reporter, "They told us when we were coming here, that we would live well. But what we saw when we got here and the way we lived here, it's the contrary. The place where we are here when it's hot, the sun makes the tents hot, very hot.

And also the wind comes and blows the tents and wrecks them".

When asked what needs to happen now, he replied, "...In the situation we're living here in the tents, we can't continue like that anymore. We would ask them as soon as possible to give us the real houses that they said they were going to give us so that our situation could improve. Because the tents are torn and when it rains, the rain comes in."

Land ownership is a particular problem for rebuilding because so many pre-quake homes were not officially registered. "Even before the national registry fell under the rubble, land tenure was always a complex and contentious issue in Haiti.

Many areas of Port-au-Prince were settled either by tonton makout – Duvalier's death squads - given land for their service or by squatters. In many cases land ownership was never officially registered.

Even if this logistical logjam were to be cleared, the vast majority of Port-au-Prince residents, up to 85%, did not own their homes before the earthquake.

In September 2010 there were over one million refugees still living in tents, and the humanitarian situation was characterized as still being in the emergency phase, according to the Apostolic Nuncio to Haiti, Archbishop Bernard Auza.

The Conclusion

He went on to say that the homeless number was rising instead of diminishing and reported that the state had decided to first rebuild downtown Port-au-Prince and a new government center, but reconstruction had not yet begun.

In October of 2010, Refugees International clearly characterized the aid agencies as dysfunctional and inexperienced saying, "The people of Haiti are still living in a state of emergency, with a humanitarian response that appears paralyzed".

It was reported that gang leaders and land owners were intimidating the displaced and that sexual, domestic, and gang violence in and around the camps was rising.

They claimed that rape of Haitian women and girls who had been living in camps since the January earthquake was increasing, in part, because the United Nations wasn't doing enough to protect them.

In October, a cholera epidemic broke out, probably introduced by foreign aid workers. Cholera most often affects poor countries with limited access to clean water and proper sanitation. By the end of 2010, more than 3,333 had died at a rate of about 50 deaths a day.

In January 2011, one year after the quake, Oxfam published a report on the status of the recovery. According to the report, relief and recovery were at a standstill due to government inaction and indecision on the part of the donor countries.

The report stated, "One year on, only five percent of the rubble has been cleared and only 15 percent of the required basic and temporary houses have been built.

House building on a large scale cannot be started before the enormous amount of rubble is cleared.

Tears of Blood

The government and donors must prioritize this most basic step toward helping people return home". Robert Fox, executive director of Oxfam Canada, said "The dysfunction has been aided unabated by the way the international community has organized itself, where pledges have been made and they haven't followed through [and] where they come to the table with their own agendas and own priorities.

Most donors provided funds for transitional housing but very little money for clearing rubble or repairing houses". Fox said that in many instances rubble removal "means it was [moved] off someone's property onto the road in front of the property".

According to a UNICEF report, "Still today more than one million people remain displaced, living in crowded camps where livelihoods, shelter and services are still hardly sufficient for children to stay healthy".

Amnesty International reported that armed men were preying with impunity on girls and women in displacement camps, worsening the trauma of having lost homes, livelihoods and loved ones.

On the first anniversary of the earthquake, Haitian-born Michaëlle Jean, who served as the Governor General of Canada at the time of the disaster and who became United Nations Educational, Scientific and Cultural Organization (UNESCO) Special Envoy for Haiti on 8 November 2010, voiced her anger at the slow rate of aid delivery, placing much of the blame on the international community for completely abandoning its commitments. In a public letter co-authored with UNESCO head Irina Bokova, Jean said, "As time passes, what began as a natural disaster is becoming a disgraceful reflection on the international community."

The Conclusion

The Interim Haiti Recovery Commission, led by former US President Bill Clinton and Haitian Prime Minister Jean-Max Bellerive, had been set up to facilitate the flow of funds toward reconstruction projects in April 2010, but as of January 2011, no major reconstruction had started.

In January 2012, two years since the quake, figures released by the United Nations show that of the nearly $4.5 billion pledged for reconstruction projects in 2010 and 2011, only 43% has been delivered.

Venezuela and the US, which promised the major share of reconstruction funds, have disbursed only 24% and 30% respectively. Japan and Finland are among the few donors to have fully met their pledges. The data shows that some crucial sectors face particularly large funding gaps. In 2010 and 2011, for example, donors disbursed just $125 million of the $311 million in grants allocated to agriculture projects, and only $108 million of the $315 million in grants allocated to health projects. Only 6% of bilateral aid for reconstruction projects has gone through Haitian institutions, and less than 1% of relief funding has gone through the government of Haiti.

A January 2012 Oxfam report said that a half a million Haitians remained homeless, still living under tarps and in tents. Watchdog groups have criticized the reconstruction process saying that part of the problem is that charities spent a considerable amount of money on "soaring rents, board members' needs, overpriced supplies and imported personnel". The Miami Herald reported. "A lot of good work was done; the money clearly didn't all get squandered," but, "A lot just wasn't responding to needs on the ground. Millions were spent on ad campaigns telling people to wash their hands.

Telling them to wash their hands when there's no water or soap is a slap in the face." The Institute of Justice & Democracy in Haiti has failed the Haitian people.

The Center for Constitutional Rights has recommended immediate changes to recovery efforts to ensure that critical human rights concerns are addressed.

A report found that, "The conditions in the displaced persons camps are abysmal, particularly for women and girls who too often are victims of gender based violence". They call for more oversight of accountability of reconstruction plans, asking, "Why have only 94,000 transitional shelters been built to date despite a stated goal of 125,000 in the first year?"

"Author's Reflection"

One has to think that there is something dreadfully wrong in the world when women and children are raped or when funds donated to a country in dire need seem to systematically vanish without a trace. This has also gone on with humanitarian help in many other parts of the world where destitute and misplaced people are cheated out of basic necessities such as food, water and medicine. When convoys with basic necessities are stolen from the starving poor in Africa or the fleeing refuges in war torn countries, then the world in its whole is going down the drain. The terrorist or highway bandits who steal these goods to sell them on the black market are nothing but despicable humanoid vultures eating on human flesh while the victims are still alive. One day all of humanity will pay for its behavior and that day may not be so far away...

Author's Reflection

What is this evil thing that makes men so wicked and cruel that they can commit such atrocities to their fellow human beings?

Dictators are killing off men, women and children as is they were nothing but left over garbage.

Terrorist are brain washing children and young adults so that they can blow themselves up and kill innocent people by the same token.

Countries with nuclear arms are getting ready to start the third world war which will destroy mankind.

All of this is happening in this new millennium when advances made by science should assure everyone a quiet and peaceful life filled with abundance for all.

But instead of pursuing the betterment of mankind, Governments only think of hanging on to their own power and wealth with a total disrespect of humanity.

Banks and institutions that grow around the banks are depriving the people of their wealth and properties thus reducing mankind to inescapable poverty.

The International Monetary Fund rules the financial world, yet none of the people within this institution are elected. Instead; they are implanted there by a secret society governed by the wealthy tyrants of the world.

There are two books, one written in 2000 and the other in 2006 that explain exactly what is going on in the world today.

They describe how the Governments and Financial institutions are systematically plundering and robbing the ordinary citizen of his rights and of his wealth.

The names of the books and where they can be found are listed on the following page.

Other books by the Author

The Soul Master Prophecies

© 2000 – ISBN # 978-0-9864825-1-9
Available at any general book store
Also on line from Amazon books
or by visiting the book's web page at
www.soulmasterprophecies.com

The Soul Master Scrolls

© 2006 – ISBN # 978-0-9864825-0-2
Available at any general book store
Also on line from Amazon books
or by visiting the book's web page at
www.soulmasterscrolls.com

From a moment in history:

'I believe that banking institutions are much more dangerous to our liberties than standing armies. If the American people ever allow private banks to control the issue of their currency, first by inflation, then by deflation, the banks and corporations that will grow up around the banks will deprive the people of all property until their children wake-up homeless on the continent their fathers conquered.'

Who wrote the above words?

They were written in 1802 by...

Thomas Jefferson, the 3 rd President

of The United States of America.

How wise he was!